D0402258

City Lights

Ministry **Essentials** for Reaching **Urban Youth**

Scott Larson and Karen Free, general editors

Loveland, Colorado

Group's R.E.A.L. Guarantee to you:

This Group resource incorporates our R.E.A.L. approach to ministry—one that encourages long-term retention and life transformation. It's ministry that's:

Relational
Because learner-to-learner interaction enhances learning and builds Christian friendships.

Experiential
Because what learners experience through discussion and action sticks with them up to 9 times longer than what they simply hear or read.

Applicable
Because the aim of Christian education is to equip learners to be both hearers and doers of God's Word.

Learner-based
Because learners understand and retain more when the learning process takes into consideration how they learn best.

City Lights:
Ministry Essentials for Reaching Urban Youth
General Editors: Scott Larson and Karen Free
Copyright © 2003 Scott Larson

All rights reserved. No part of this book may be reproduced in any manner whatsoever without prior written permission from the publisher, except where noted in the text and in the case of brief quotations embodied in critical articles and reviews. For information write Permissions, Group Publishing, Inc., Dept. PD, P.O. Box 481, Loveland, CO 80539.

Visit our Web site: **www.grouppublishing.com**

Credits
General Editors: Scott Larson and Karen Free
Contributing Authors: Rev. Alvin C. Bibbs Sr., Dean Borgman, Harvey F. Carey, Patricia Coleman Hill, Marvin A. Daniels, Ken Gordon, Charles Harper, Rev. Eli V. Hernandez, Chris Hill, Rudy Howard, Judy D. Landis, Dr. Scott Larson, Efrem Smith, Rev. Claire Sullivan, Chris Troy, Harold Dean Trulear, Joel Van Dyke, Peter Vanacore, and Karin M. Wall, LICSW
Editor: Amy Simpson
Creative Development Editor: Dave Thornton
Chief Creative Officer: Joani Schultz
Copy Editor: Loma Huh
Art Director: Kari K. Monson
Cover Art Director: Jeff A. Storm
Cover Designer: Blukazoo Studio
Print Production Artist: Tracy K. Donaldson
Illustrator: Stephen Marchesi
Production Manager: Dodie Tipton

Unless otherwise noted, Scripture taken from the HOLY BIBLE, NEW INTERNATIONAL VERSION®. Copyright © 1973, 1978, 1984 by International Bible Society. Used by permission of Zondervan Publishing House. All rights reserved.

Library of Congress Cataloging-in-Publication Data
City lights : ministry essentials for reaching urban youth / general editors, Scott Larson and Karen Free.
    p. cm.
  Includes bibliographical references.
  ISBN 0-7644-2386-X (pbk. : alk. paper)
    1. Church work with teenagers. 2. Church work with minorities. 3. City churches. I. Larson, Scott, 1959- II. Free, Karen.
BV4447 .C49 2002
259'.23'091732--dc21   2002011508

10 9 8 7 6 5 4 3 2 1   12 11 10 09 08 07 06 05 04 03
Printed in the United States of America.

Contributing Authors

Rev. Alvin C.
Bibbs Sr.

Dean Borgman

Harvey F. Carey

Patricia Coleman Hill
and Judy D. Landis

Marvin A. Daniels

Ken Gordon

Charles Harper

Rev. Eli V.
Hernandez

Chris Hill

Rudy Howard

Dr. Scott Larson

Efrem Smith

Rev. Claire
Sullivan

Chris Troy

Harold Dean
Trulear

Joel Van Dyke

Peter Vanacore   Kathy McWhirt

CONCORDIA UNIVERSITY LIBRARY
PORTLAND. OR 97211

Contributing Authors Biographies

Rev. Alvin C. Bibbs Sr.—Rev. Alvin C. Bibbs Sr. is director of extension ministries at Willow Creek Community Church in South Barrington, Illinois. Rev. Bibbs also works as a chaplain with professional sports teams in Chicago. He has a master of arts degree in Christian leadership development from Fuller Theological Seminary. Alvin is married to Peggy, and they have two sons: Alvin Cartel Jr. and Brandon Quintin.

Dean Borgman—Dean Borgman is professor of youth ministry and holds the Charles E. Culpeper Chair of Youth Ministry at Gordon-Conwell Theological Seminary's urban campus in Boston, Massachusetts. He is also founder and director of the Center for Youth Studies, a national and global network of those interested in research on adolescence and the youth culture. Dean has written several books and articles on youth culture and youth ministry. He earned a master of arts degree in education at Fairfield University. Dean and his wife, Gail, have four children: John, Debbie, Matthew, and Christen.

Harvey F. Carey—Harvey F. Carey is assistant pastor at Salem Baptist Church of Chicago in Chicago, Illinois. Rev. Carey is known for his remarkable ability to communicate the transforming Word of God to people of all ages. He has served as a contributing author for books about youth ministry. He is pursuing his master of divinity degree at Trinity Evangelical Divinity School. He and his wife, Nancy, have one daughter, Tiffany.

Patricia Coleman Hill—Patricia Coleman Hill is director of the M.O.D.E.L. (Made of Divine Excellence and Love) Mentoring Program at Freedom Christian Bible Fellowship in Philadelphia, Pennsylvania. The M.O.D.E.L. program helps young ladies in the public school system with disciplinary problems and helps them turn their lives around through one-on-one mentoring. Patricia also operates her own family catering business. She has one daughter, Keita Nwenna.

Marvin A. Daniels—Marvin A. Daniels is Midwest regional program facilitator with Compassion USA, and lives in Chicago, Illinois. Compassion USA is a Christian child advocacy ministry that assists local churches and Christian ministries in building developmental holistic programs for at-risk and impoverished children and youth in America's inner cities, rural South, and American Indian reservations. Marvin has been a youth minister for fourteen years in various urban centers in America. He is married to LeAndra Letrese and has four children: Malachi, Isaiah, Micah, and Imani.

Ken Gordon—Ken Gordon is pastor of Lowell Mission Church in Lowell, Massachusetts. He has been an officer in the local organization Cambodian American Christian Fellowship, which seeks to enhance fellowship and evangelistic outreach within the local Cambodian community. He holds a bachelor of science degree in cross-cultural studies from North Central Bible College. He and his wife, Rhea, have three children: Kendra, Caleb, and Daniel.

Charles Harper—Charles Harper is director of Christ for Native Youth and lives in Albuquerque, New Mexico. He has served in Native ministry for eighteen years in Alaska, Arizona, and New Mexico. Charles is a graduate of Moody Bible Institute, Columbia College, and Biblical Theological Seminary. He is married to Cindy and has three sons.

Rev. Eli V. Hernandez—Rev. Eli V. Hernandez is pastor of Iglesia Bautista Central in Orlando, Florida, and founder of Breath of Life Outreach Ministries, which focuses on at-risk youth. He also serves as the youth consultant for the American Baptist denomination in Florida. As an evangelist and motivational speaker, he ministers to thousands of youth and families around the country and abroad. He has written several articles on street and hip-hop culture and Hispanic youth ministry. Rev. Hernandez is a candidate for a master of divinity degree from Gordon-Conwell Theological Seminary. He is married to Rev. Aprilis Y. Diaz-Hernandez and has a daughter, Suheily.

Chris Hill—Chris Hill is youth pastor and associate pastor of The Potter's House in Dallas, Texas. Having served as an urban youth pastor, evangelist, and motivational speaker for nearly twenty years, Pastor Hill has great success in motivating people to improve their lives spiritually, educationally, socially, and economically. He is the author of *The Winning Spirit* (Group Publishing). Chris is married to Lady Joy Hill, and they have a son, Christopher Hill Jr.

Rudy Howard—Rudy Howard is president and founder of Luke 4:18 Ministries in Memphis, Tennessee. As executive director of the Urban Youth Initiative in Memphis, Rev. Howard recruited, funded, trained, and deployed over eighty urban youth leaders to reach unchurched young people. Rev. Howard holds master of arts and master of divinity degrees from Fuller Theological Seminary. He and his wife, Kathy, have one son, Christian.

Judy D. Landis—Judy D. Landis coordinates the urban missions ministry of Freedom Christian Bible Fellowship in Philadelphia, Pennsylvania. Judy has served as a conference and retreat speaker, addressing economic and racial justice concerns. She has also taught urban youth ministry courses at Eastern College and Eastern Baptist Theological Seminary. She holds a master's degree in urban missions from Westminster Theological Seminary.

Dr. Scott Larson—Rev. Dr. Scott Larson is president and founder of Straight Ahead Ministries in Westboro, Massachusetts. Straight Ahead Ministries is a national organization focused on reaching juvenile offenders. Scott has authored six books (including *At Risk* and *Risk in Our Midst* with Group Publishing) and has traveled extensively as a speaker to youth, parents, teachers, social workers, and youth workers since 1983. Scott and his wife, Hanne, have two children, Sarah and David.

Efrem Smith—Efrem Smith is youth pastor at Park Avenue Church and executive director of Park Avenue Foundation in Minneapolis, Minnesota. Efrem has been a featured speaker at events such as Soul Liberation Festival, Extreme 98, Hoodfest, Cornerstone Festival, and Athletes in Action. He has also provided workshops for Youth Leadership, Campus Crusade for Christ, and Youth Specialties. Raised in Minneapolis, Efrem is a graduate of Minneapolis North High School, St. John's University, and Luther Theological Seminary. He and his wife, Donecia, have two daughters, Jaeda and Mireya.

Rev. Claire Sullivan—Rev. Claire Sullivan is a missionary at Emmanuel Gospel Center and a licensed minister at Lion of Judah Church in Roxbury, Massachusetts. She is also Boston coordinator for Straight Ahead Ministries. Claire founded and directed Starlight Ministries, an interdenominational outreach to Boston's homeless. She holds a master of arts degree in urban ministry from Gordon-Conwell Theological Seminary.

Chris Troy—Chris Troy is founder and president of the Boston Urban Youth Foundation in Boston, Massachusetts. The Boston Urban Youth Foundation serves over 500 young people with the mission of "helping young people develop spiritually, emotionally, academically, and economically." Chris is a graduate of Bethel College and has a long history of being committed to seeing at-risk youth living the abundant life of Christ.

Harold Dean Trulear—Harold Dean Trulear is pastor of Mount Pleasant Baptist Church of Twin Oaks, Pennsylvania. He also teaches religion, public policy, and community studies at several institutions, including Yale University,

Drew University, Hartford Seminary, Eastern College, and the Center for Urban Theological Studies. Dr. Trulear serves on several boards and has authored more than sixty published articles, essays, sermons, and reviews. He recently completed a three-year stint as vice president of faith-based initiatives at Public/Private Ventures, a policy think tank in Philadelphia. Dr. Trulear is a graduate of Morehouse College and holds a doctorate from Drew University. He and his wife, Vickie, are the parents of three adolescent children.

Joel Van Dyke—Joel Van Dyke is senior pastor of Bethel Temple Community Bible Church in Philadelphia, Pennsylvania. In addition, he has worked with the Compassionworks Urban Youth Workers Conference as conference planner and trainer since its inception in 1989. He also developed and directed a citywide student leadership program for the Philadelphia Project for Youth Ministry. Joel has a master of divinity degree, with a special emphasis in urban missions, from Westminster Theological Seminary. He and his wife, Marilyn, have a son, Joeito.

Peter Vanacore—Peter Vanacore is national field director for Straight Ahead Ministries in Westboro, Massachusetts. Peter has lectured at various colleges and seminaries on crisis intervention, ministry to troubled youth, and child abuse intervention. Peter has a masters in social work from Fordham University. He is married to Dianne and has three children: Sarah, Kirk, and Mark.

Karin M. Wall, LICSW—Karin M. Wall is executive director of Bruce Wall Ministries in Boston, Massachusetts. She is also a licensed independent clinical social worker. For Karin, working with youth is a means to an end—it ultimately produces healthy adults. She holds master's degrees in social work and African American history, both from Boston University. She is married to Bruce, and they have three children.

Contents

Foreword
By George Gallup Jr.

t's a national shame: America has virtually abandoned many youth in our cities to lives of hopelessness and despair. While many programs have made impressive headway in reaching inner-city families, a great deal more needs to be done to give urban youth new hope for the future.

Youth are ignored at great peril, and in this respect it is helpful to take a brief look at the world of teenagers, as we have sought to discern it through ongoing surveys of teenagers over the last quarter century.

Teenagers do not see the future in glowing terms. Many feel physically unsafe on the street, in school, even in their own homes.

It's no exaggeration to say that we are a society in risk of losing a generation. Youth are threatened on all sides by problems relatively new to the scene: AIDS and other sexual diseases, exotic and mind-altering drugs and alcohol, sophisticated weapons that belong only in the hands of the military, and random acts of violence.

U.S. teenagers take a rather dim view of the condition of their world and their future in it. A majority of teenagers say they believe the world they are growing up in now is worse than the one their parents knew when they were young.

Sizeable numbers of teenagers expect that some of life's most distressing experiences will happen to them, with a majority expecting to one day be the victim of some form of crime. Nearly half think they will be mugged. As many as one-third say it is likely that a violent crime will befall them, such as being shot or stabbed.

Teenagers are also somber when projecting ahead to their personal relationships. Four in ten feel it is at least somewhat likely that a future marriage for them will end in divorce. (They are not far off the mark—some estimates are that every other marriage today will break up.)

Sadly, adults too often view teenagers in a negative light and overlook the truly positive characteristics of youth today. For example, large majorities of young people report that they are happy and excited about the future, feel very close to their families, say they are likely to marry, want to have children, are satisfied with their personal lives, are generally happy with who they are, and desire to reach the top of their chosen careers.

But all of this is in jeopardy if our society does not give full attention to the youth culture of today. And front and center in this effort should be the churches of our nation.

It is a great blessing that the United States, unlike most other nations of the world, has the church infrastructure to reach urban youth on a major scale with the life-transforming message of the gospel of Jesus Christ. There are an estimated 350,000 churches in this nation, reaching a solid 60 percent of the population in any given month.

With a sense of urgency, churches of all denominations need to examine their youth ministries and ask basic questions relating to their mission: Do youth programs have high priority? Are congregants encouraged to move out of their comfort zones and engage in hands-on, face-to-face interaction with youth in need? What outreach programs should we consider?

Congregations need to develop new partnerships not only with other churches, but also with other organizations, both nonprofit and profit, to bring social health to their communities. More can be done to encourage "sister church" programs. For example, more affluent churches can reach out to less affluent ones—coming together not only in worship services but in small groups, as well as other exchanges.

There is great need to focus with a laser beam on youth in the inner city. The focus of churches, however, should extend to urban youth in general—indeed, to the whole youth population—for the fact is, in many churches youth programs are either faltering or nonexistent.

The future vigor and health of our churches, of Christianity in general, and indeed of society as a whole, depend in considerable measure on what churches are willing to do today to provide a setting that changes young people's lives through knowledge of Jesus Christ.

We cannot ignore the spiritual dimensions of the problems and promise of youth. A growing body of survey evidence shows that religious faith can literally save a young person's life. A growing mountain of data shows that religious faith and church connections play a decisive role in the lives of youth. Youth with this background tend to be happy and more goal-oriented, do better in school, are less likely to get into trouble, and are more likely to serve others. In addition, many more churchgoing than non-churchgoing teenagers say they always see a reason for their being here on earth.

In the inner city, churches and youth ministries are often the only institutions that still work. To fail to give teenagers and preteens full attention at this time of their profound spiritual need, is to store up problems for all generations to come.

One can, I believe, make a strong case that the focus of churches at this point in the nation's history should be relentlessly on ministry to urban youth, particularly in view of two important demographic facts: (1) More than half of the world's population lives in cities, with cities in the United States continuing to swell; and (2) approximately 40 percent of the world's population is nineteen or younger, with the "millennial generation" in the United States including more children and youth in school than any other cohort in U.S. history.

Before churches take on the challenging task of developing a courageous and faith-driven ministry to urban youth, it is vital that they know the territory. Therefore, this remarkable new book is making a timely appearance. *City Lights* is a compilation of insightful articles on the key aspects of urban youth ministry. This book offers great insight into the urban youth culture and provides a blueprint for this vital ministry.

Every base is covered in these chapters by writers who not only have solid academic backgrounds but who have firsthand experience in dealing with urban youth, including inner-city kids. We learn about different strategies that are needed for different groups, the pros and cons of mentoring, the steps needed to train youth leaders, how parents can be encouraged to get into the act, and how to help young people make the transition from the street to church. And the list goes on.

City Lights is a basic primer for urban youth ministry. It is a vital book for our day, because churches will be focal in the recovery of societal health.

Will the churches of America, as we look to the future, be effective in moving members out of their comfort zones to take on the difficult and demanding work that Jesus Christ has called us to undertake—reaching "the lost" and "the least" in the cities of America?

The challenges are huge, but so are the opportunities. Urban youth, like youth all across the nation, are searching for spiritual moorings with a new intensity. There is a widespread hunger for God.

Indeed, the wonderful prospect arises that if we treat urban youth not as pathologies but as sparks of joy and beloved children of God, these transformed youth could well be on the leading edge of renewal in the years ahead. We can be certain that God has very special plans for America's urban youth.

Introduction

For too long, urban ministries have had to adapt materials to their needs because of the lack of materials targeted specifically for urban youth. This is completely backward—most trends originate in urban communities before becoming part of mainstream youth culture in five to ten years. In fact, because of worldwide technology and the globalization of youth culture, the span of time this "mainstreaming" takes is shortening all the time.

Many people, for example, don't realize that school violence was not invented in 1996 when Barry Loukaitis fatally shot one teacher and two students in Moses Lake, Washington. In the 1992–1993 school year, fifty people were murdered in public schools, but because those murders occurred primarily in urban settings and involved low-income minority youth, the public outcry was much less pronounced.[1]

Through the influence of the global hip-hop subculture, American inner-city teenagers are actually leading youth culture at large. But this is the case not only in clothing styles and music. Urban youth are also poised to lead teenagers worldwide toward Christ, as they become radically committed to him.

Common sense would say we ought to be investing a good share of our curriculum development dollars in urban youth programs. Innovative programs that are successful in our cities today will be our most effective programs for reaching mainstream rural and suburban youth in just a few short years.

City Lights: Ministry Essentials for Reaching Urban Youth contains the most cutting-edge urban youth ministry models in America today. Not mere theorists, the authors of these eighteen chapters are on the front lines, ministering to urban teens from virtually every culture and subculture in our inner cities. This book covers every aspect of the complex ministry of reaching kids in urban America. It is invaluable for those who feel called to leave the suburbs for the city, as well as for veterans who have labored with urban kids for years. It's been our distinct privilege to work with each of these authors as we have attempted to pull out the best of what they have learned in a collective four hundred–plus years of frontline urban youth ministry.

Enjoy it. But above all—and for the sake of thousands of kids—put it into practice!

Scott Larson

Endnote

[1] James Garbarino, Ph.D., *Lost Boys* (New York, NY: The Free Press, 1999), 16.

Chapter 1
A Philosophy of Urban Youth Ministry

Harold Dean Trulear

There is a critical tension inherent in any discussion on contemporary philosophy of urban ministry. This tension arises at least partly out of a confusion surrounding the definition of the term *urban*. Historic sociological analysis has always considered the city as a richly textured, multilayered political, social, and cultural entity. Contemporary Christianity, though, has come to define *urban* as a small slice of the city—namely, the so-called "inner city."

When I was team-teaching at a theological seminary in the northeast several years ago, my colleague presented an impassioned lecture on the need for the urban church to minister to the poor and the outcast, to advocate for the voiceless and provide services for the marginalized.

When the lecture was over, a student approached me in the hallway and said, "If that's urban ministry, then where do I live? I'm a certified public accountant and I live in a middle-class community in the heart of the city, but according to your definition of urban ministry, I'm not urban. Do you have to be a poor minority to be urban?"

My response consisted of repentance. I realized that I myself held a stereotypical, even stigmatizing, perspective on the city. Urban ministry had come to represent going to those dark, difficult, despairing places of need. My youth ministry training had taught me to "bring Christ to the city," where "he is needed most."

A Metropolitan Ministry

If we move to a philosophy of "metropolitan ministry," we change the lens and broaden the focus. Metropolitan ministry recognizes three important realities. First, the city, including its inner-city and poor neighborhoods, exists as part of a larger *social system*, and contains within its borders a variety of smaller, interrelated institutions. These systems and institutions interconnect with and influence each other as they regularly make decisions that inform, influence, and almost control the lives of a variety of people across the metropolitan area. They include economic, educational, political, health care, family, communications, and even religious institutions.

Second, youth ministers are not exempt from a misunderstanding of urban ministry. Metropolitan ministry forces the youth minister to regular self-examination: What are my prejudices and presuppositions? Where did they come from? Do I unknowingly stereotype races and cultures?

In other words, we must move beyond viewing urban youth ministry as merely "working with inner-city kids," toward understanding the vast complex of institutions that make up the metropolis. Then, inevitably we will be led to cry out to God for forgiveness for our complicity in developing and benefiting from the way those systems work, as well as to regular periods of self-examination concerning our motives for "doing" youth ministry.

Third, our look beyond stigmatized people and neighborhoods to this broader picture brings us to a surprising conclusion. If, in fact, "the system" has a detrimental effect on the lives of urban, even inner-city, youth (such as a lack of affordable housing and jobs that pay a living wage), and if we are benefiting from and contributing to that system, then it is theologically impossible to argue that we "bring Jesus to poor and distressed neighborhoods."

When we understand the complexity of the city and the problems that exist at virtually every level, we are led to an interesting paradox. Christ is needed everywhere in the city, and Christ is present everywhere in the city. The challenge is not *to bring* Christ to inner-city youth, but rather *to meet* Christ wherever he is in this vast complex and to cooperate with him in his ministry wherever he calls and leads.

The work of H. Paul Douglass, Frederick Shippey, and other scholars of the urban church has done a good job documenting ministry with city youth from the turn of the century through the 1960s. But beginning in the late sixties and early seventies, urban unrest and inner-city problems began to attract a new generation of urban missioners. Their work, while noble, sometimes ignored both the history and the tradition of urban youth ministry and, perhaps more important, the ongoing work of indigenous congregations and ministries that had faithfully persisted through times of rapid social change.

The focus of literature on urban youth ministry over the past thirty years has documented a new breed of missionaries: parachurch workers, denominational missionaries, and urban youth specialists. While their important contributions to the kingdom are to be celebrated, they must also be subjected to more critical sociological and theological analysis.

This same literature has also been thin in chronicling the work of indigenous churches. This does not discredit the work of the missionary; rather, it calls for a refocusing of urban youth ministry in light of the existing traditions and available resources in indigenous congregations and ministries. This shift in perspective enables us to more clearly see the full orbit of urban youth ministry, as opposed to reducing its existence to a series of missionary endeavors.

Critical Issues for Successful Inner-City Youth Ministry

In 2000, I authored a report entitled "Faith-Based Institutions and High Risk Youth." It was the first report of several explaining research findings of a study conducted by Public/Private Ventures, a national nonprofit organization whose mission is to improve the effectiveness of social policies, programs, and community initiatives, especially as they affect youth and young adults.

The information developed for this report confirmed much of what I had learned in my work as a youth minister in churches and organizations in Philadelphia and in Paterson, N.J., as well as observations made in twenty years of working with and training urban youth workers. In addition, I had opportunity to view a variety of ministries across the country that were not included in the study but showed great creativity in the development of partnerships with government and other agencies in a systemic approach to ministry with city youth and their families. These are all critical elements for successful youth ministry in the urban context.

While the ministries observed in the study focused primarily on high-risk youth and the reduction of juvenile crime, the lessons learned have a broader applicability to urban youth ministry as a whole. Life in the city simply makes the problems of youth more visible by virtue of the close proximity of institutions to each other, and the density of population that affords few places to hide. Focusing on the essential elements for successful ministry to high-risk youth, then, becomes a lens through which we can view best practices for the field of urban youth ministry as a whole. I have listed six such characteristics that I believe frame a healthy philosophy for any urban youth ministry. While each of these is fleshed out in more depth in subsequent chapters, for now let's just take a broader look at the some of the unique challenges and innovative approaches present in some of today's most effective inner-city youth ministries.

1. The Challenge of Targeting High-Risk Youth

Traditional public and nonprofit youth programs do not reach most high-risk youth in poor communities primarily because there are few, if any, programs specifically targeting such youth.[1] Many inner-city ministries target neighborhoods in their outreach. Most churches reflect a parish approach to urban ministry, focusing on communities as the primary repository of social and community life. These congregations rightly feel a sense of responsibility for community wholeness and well-being. But youth programs and ministries that target neighborhoods cast a broad net, reasoning, "Whosoever will, let them come."

When churches and agencies offer such a general invitation, however, they tend to attract the youth who are already looking for some type of guidance—or at least a respite from the pressures of life in their communities. But here's the crucial point: Many times, targeting a community's youth without specifying a strategy that addresses the identification and recruitment of high-risk youth leads to a program that works with the good kids in a bad neighborhood. Pointing to "success" rates among such youth amounts to a form of bait-and-switch ministry.

While the parish approach is necessary, noble, and critical to the development of that particular group of teenagers who need love, support, and a way to navigate life, our ministries must be discerning in identifying the *most difficult* youth (high-risk youth), as opposed to merely at-risk youth. Here's the difference: High-risk youth are those youth who are already involved in criminal and violent activities or who have been deemed likely candidates for such behavior by neighborhood residents, agencies, school officials, or community leaders. At-risk kids are those who need attention, as they might *become* something negative.[2] Spending time in our communities getting to know who's who among neighborhood youth is an indispensable component of outreach, and gives us a more accurate picture of what our ministry is, or should be, all about.

2. The Need for Focused Leadership

Congregations in distressed urban communities are often called upon to meet a variety of legitimate needs. Pastors, ministers, and other church leaders regularly respond to requests for counseling, food, clothing, and shelter from the poor in their midst. As a result, such needs naturally become the driving force behind community service and consume most, if not all, of a congregation's human-service capacity.

When governed by the tyranny of need, however, congregations become fragmented in their approach to service, stretched to the limits of their resources and often plagued by an unsystematic delivery system. In responding to the immediacy of crises before them, many faith-based organizations' allocations of resources lead to shortfalls in other areas, weaken the ongoing infrastructure of the congregation's community service system, and lead to burnout. Focusing solely on individual needs also keeps a congregation from seeing the big picture—the systemic picture.

Programs that avoid such fragmentation and burnout are characterized by focused leadership—pastors and congregational leaders who have determined that they will be driven by specific initiatives rather than general needs. They do not attempt to be all things to all people. For some congregations, this means filtering all ministries through a lens that focuses on the particular need being addressed.[3] This lens enables the ministry to address all of the systemic issues attendant to the issue, that is, the various institutions impacting youth, the family of the youth, and the community environment. As a result, one-on-one ministry joins with advocacy in a partnership that is far more holistic.

3. The Challenge of Capacity Building

Most congregations and faith-based organizations that are focused on and effective in reaching high-risk youth tend to be small (averaging between 50 and 200 members), and personality-driven.[4] In other words, the outreach is usually effective because it is directly tied to a person who is naturally gifted in relating to and impacting highly troubled teenagers.

The challenge then becomes figuring out how to replicate this strategy so that it is less dependent upon a person and more applicable as a model for others to incarnate—a process that many "direct ministry" types aren't always open to, as they often reason that "no one else can relate with these kids the way I can." Yet this essential process of "institutionalizing" an effective model is critical for any ministry to high-risk youth to be widespread and sustaining.

Often, cooperation between ministry organizations and churches, especially smaller congregations, can serve to build capacity. In some cases, an intermediary organization can provide the necessary infrastructure for cooperation. These organizations serve to strengthen ministries through technical assistance, networking, and training. Sometimes this is done through offering courses, seminars, and other public or constituent-driven events. At other times, the intermediary may contract with individual ministries to provide such services.

These intermediaries can also facilitate collaboration between ministries and government and other institutions, acting as contacts or even fiscal agents for ministries receiving government funding. Sometimes they even work to help secure government contracts (foundation grants and/or other financial resources) and subcontract with ministries for specific services to young people. These intermediaries absorb the administrative strain of dealing with the bureaucratic demands of accountability for resources and programs to agencies who rightly expect responsibility from organizations "on the ground" who are ministering with their resources.

4. The Need for Collaboration

One key way a ministry can build capacity is to forge strategic relationships with other institutions that impact the lives of youth. A willingness to collaborate with other congregations and community organizations, law enforcement, and educational institutions adds great benefit to any ministry trying to meet the complex needs of high-risk youth. When a faith-based organization intentionally chooses to do one thing well, it must create relationships both with agencies that help accomplish that focused task and with those who can help with the other tasks of ministry that cannot go unattended. For example, some youth ministries receive referrals directly from their communities' juvenile justice agencies. Others divert nonviolent first offenders into mentoring relationships with church laypeople as an alternative to detention or lockup. As part of that, youth may be incorporated into existing church programs such as after-school tutorial or job readiness programs.

One such partnership is the GRACE program in Detroit, which made its focus high-risk youth on the streets. This program was started by a youth pastor and former gang member. His past had equipped him to learn who was who on the street and to be an available presence to recruit those seeking to leave gang life. With the help of his parish, he negotiated a truce with the neighborhood gangs. The gang leaders told him that if he took kids out of the gangs he would need to offer them something better: education and employment. As of early 1999, GRACE had served nearly 250 youth, ages eighteen to twenty-four, with no episodes of recidivism and a greater than 90 percent job-retention rate.[5]

Cooperative strategies enable the small, focused congregation to multiply resources and develop relationships that allow it to maximize its efficiency in delivering services to high-risk youth. But collaboration must extend beyond just urban youth and affect their families as well. Families of high-risk youth often exist somewhere between the ranks of the overlooked (we don't see them) and the demonized (they failed their kids—so the urban youth minister must fill the gap) in our theology of urban youth ministry.

5. Building Relationships of Trust

Effective programming alone does not make for successful outreach. A 1990 study of effective programs in the nation's prisons concludes that having the right personnel in place is more crucial to effective programming than is program content.[6]

The difference that caring adults make in the lives of young people has been widely documented through studies of mentoring programs such as Big Brothers Big Sisters of America, the GRACE program mentioned earlier, and many others. All share a commitment to mobilizing a significant number of adults to mentor or befriend youth in need of caring adults in their lives—adults they can trust.

Trust is the basis for significant relationship building with high-risk youth. Developing a trustworthy relationship is critically important as part of a strategy for gaining knowledge of who's who in the community in general and within the urban youth subculture in particular. Building relationships with a difficult-to-reach population takes time, on the streets as well as during program hours. Time on the streets involves developing a presence in the neighborhood sufficient to identify and win the trust of high-risk youth.

In the Azusa Christian Community and its Ella J. Baker House in the Dorchester section of Boston, Pastor Eugene Rivers has successfully directed the energies of his congregation to a focus on youth and "taking back the streets" through relationship building. He, along with other ministers and church leaders, conducted weekly Friday night street patrols. For the first six months, very few people talked to them. When conversations did develop, according to Rev. Rivers, the street patrol members did not preach. Rather, they asked how they, as churches and church leaders, could be of service to the youth—offering counsel, job and educational opportunities, and other sound alternatives to life on the street. The key, says Rivers, is that when offering help, you are able to deliver.

6. The Role of Faith

I dare say that few would possess any desire to work with at-risk and high-risk youth if faith was not their primary motivation. Faith-motivated volunteers draw tremendous strength from their sense of mission; they see faith as that which enables them to do the difficult work of ministering to underserved youth, to take the time necessary to develop relationships of trust and accountability, and to endure the struggles and setbacks that inevitably come when youth "fall away" or become recidivists. Faith becomes the impetus for caring.

Early findings from the Public/Private Ventures initiative suggest that in order for high-risk youth to reach the goals of avoiding violence, achieving literacy, and accessing jobs, they must experience a transformation of values that reorders their sense of meaning and purpose in life.[7] Vibrant congregations are places where the deeper questions of life can be explored, especially in the context of relationships with adults who, motivated by their faith, truly care about struggling teenagers.

We all need some form of meaning system to navigate life's journey. The faith community offers such a moral compass to high-risk youth. Ideally, it is one of the few places where such young people can find caring adults to share their faith with youth—not through sermonizing or confrontational means, but rather through relational methods that can accept young people where they are, but point them toward a more positive hope and a future (Jeremiah 29:11).

To summarize, urban youth ministry involves more than just working with inner-city kids. You must discern before God how he would have you adequately address the impact of the whole city, but then focus on that part that he's calling you to. As you do that, your ministry to urban youth may then call you to work with the families of these young people as well. It may require you to labor within the world of your area's current political decision makers too. It may also involve working with the teenagers of that certified public accountant I mentioned earlier, who may well join the future ranks of the decision makers and may need someone to sensitize them now to their responsibility in Christ for stewardship of the city.

In each case, Christ calls us to his ministry, which is found in all kinds of places within the metropolitan area.

Endnotes

(Portions of the article "Faith-Based Institutions and High-Risk Youth: First Report to the Field," from the *Field Report Series* published in 2000 by Public/Private Ventures, are incorporated in this article, reprinted with the permission of Public/Private Ventures.)

[1] Harold Dean Trulear, "Faith-Based Institutions and High-Risk Youth: First Report to the Field," *Field Report Series* (Philadelphia: Public/Private Ventures: Spring 2000), 1. Used by permission of Public/Private Ventures.

[2] Ibid., 11.

[3] Ibid., 10.

[4] Ibid., 7.

[5] Ibid., 14.

[6] Ibid., 15.

[7] Ibid., 17.

Chapter 2
Communicating the Gospel in an Urban Context

Efrem Smith

oes God have a word for urban youth? Is there anything from ancient Israel that today's urban teenagers can relate to? The answers are yes and yes! Throughout the Bible we read stories of God using young people in incredible ways.

In 1 Samuel God used a boy named David to take down a giant named Goliath. In 2 Kings, a boy named Josiah became king at eight years of age and brought God-honoring reform to an entire nation! The book of Jeremiah chronicles the story of a boy who thought he was too young to make a difference. God is in the business of using young people to change the world.

Consider the story of Timothy in the book of Acts. When Paul met Timothy, he discovered that his mother was a Christian but his father was not. While growing up, I knew many young people whose mothers would drag them to church while dad stayed home to watch a game on TV. The story of Timothy speaks directly to the issues many urban young people deal with every day of their lives.

The book of Esther contains the story of a girl who became a queen and then was used by God to bring spiritual, political, and social renewal to her land and people. In the beginning of the book we discover that Esther never knew her biological mother or father and was raised by a cousin. She also had to keep her true nationality a secret because her people were treated like second-class citizens.

Basically, Esther was a foster child and a person of color. Presenting truths like this is essential, as most urban young people assume that all Bible characters are white. This should not be surprising, as it's how most biblical movies and children's lessons have portrayed them.

Rather than some foreign document far removed from the issues, challenges, and barriers that today's urban youth face on a daily basis, in actuality the Bible speaks to urban young people through many powerful and relevant stories. When such truths are taught this way, the Bible becomes a powerful tool that brings transformation to the minds, spirits, and bodies of urban teenagers.

The question is, do *we* see Scripture this way? Do we recognize the Bible as the most multi-ethnic piece of literature ever written? When we read the Bible do we see the faces of the urban young people around us? Do we see ourselves as those necessary vehicles to bring the voice of God through Scripture to today's urban young people right where they are?

Ministering in an Urban Context

The city is an exciting place to communicate the gospel of Jesus Christ for a number of reasons, but let me focus on one: ethnic diversity. In South Minneapolis, where I minister, understanding how to communicate the gospel among ethnically diverse people groups is a major issue. Based on 2000 census data, our state's nonwhite population increased sharply from 1990 to 1996: The population of African Americans rose 33 percent; Asians, 41 percent; American Indians, almost 12 percent; Hispanics, 40 percent; Caucasians, nearly 5 percent.[1]

But such traditional demographic data classes do not even account for growing people groups like the Somali and Hmong communities in my neighborhood. For example, the Hmong population in Minnesota has doubled in the last decade with the majority of that population residing in urban communities.[2] This growth in ethnic diversity is happening across the United States.

So how does the Bible speak to communities that look like these? Actually, ethnic diversity was foundational at the very launching of the church. In Acts 2 we see how on the day of Pentecost, the Spirit of God moved within a very multi-ethnic population of people. The Scriptures record that these multi-ethnic people heard the apostles speaking in their native languages. When Peter proclaimed the gospel, three thousand of them believed, and their lives were forever transformed. Thus, the first Christian church was a multi-ethnic community of Christians who couldn't even understand each other's mother languages!

Reaching Urban Youth

I didn't become a Christian through a Sunday morning church service, a large youth conference, or a television evangelist, but through Joey, a high school classmate. He shared Jesus with me on the school bus to Minneapolis North Community High School. Joey was not ordained, seminary trained, or even an adult. But he saw himself as a voice for God in my high school. Many young people became Christians through the ministry of this inner-city young person.

Joey was effective because he communicated the gospel of Jesus Christ at our level. Perhaps because he was a kid like us, and didn't come across as a religious know-it-all, we were more open to listening to him. But in order for Jocy to see himself this way, someone had to speak into his life. That person was Bart Campolo, Joey's youth pastor at the time.

Bart had a way of communicating the gospel of Jesus Christ to urban youth that made it come alive. When he read the Bible he saw similarities between the characters of the Bible and the urban young people around him. As a result, he was able to speak to Joey in a way that helped him see himself as one of those people who could be used by God to change the world.

Effectively communicating the gospel to urban teenagers demands that we first recognize how God used young people in Scripture, and then translate that to our teenagers, helping them gain a vision for how God wants to use them.

See As God Sees

Communicating the gospel to urban teenagers begins with possessing a passion for them. We must be able to see beyond their faults and struggles to what they can become. Many people miss opportunities to speak a transforming message into the lives of urban youth because they speak only to what they see with the natural eye. If all you see is a gang member, school dropout, or troublemaker, you speak words of shame and not of transformation. We must learn to see urban youth through the eyes of God if we're to communicate a transforming message. We must speak to where urban youth are as well as to what they can become. This is how God speaks to young people.

In the story of young David recorded in 1 Samuel, the natural eye would conclude, "David, you're the last son, and that means within your culture you aren't going to amount to much." But the eyes of God saw a giant-slayer. So

God began to prepare David, not to be last, but to be first among warriors. He empowered David to kill the lion and the bear that attacked the sheep he was assigned to. In killing the lion and the bear, David was being prepared for the other "giants" that would enter his life.

We must communicate a message to urban youth that prepares them for what they can become. We must teach with words that prepare them for the giant issues of marriage, entrepreneurship, compassion, and strategic think-ing. We must speak a transforming message that begins with their potential.

What do you see when you look at urban youth? Do you see problems? Do you see trouble? Or you do you see potential young heroes with the gifts and abilities to change the world? This is a major issue both within and outside the church. Most of us have poor eyesight when it comes to looking at our urban youth. It's critical that we get a vision beyond our natural eye for the youth of our cities, and begin praying for them that way.

If we fail to communicate a message of transformation to urban youth, other voices will be there to take our place. Urban young people are attacked daily by media and entertainment voices attempting to influence them to paths that are far from the plan God has for their lives. Because there are not enough voices presenting the gospel at a level where urban youth can know that God has a word specifically for them, many teenagers are listening and responding to voices that lead them to choices that bring pain, setbacks, and sometimes death.

At this point you may be thinking, "Wait a minute, there are lots of churches in the city where urban youth can hear a word from God, aren't there?"

The answer is a resounding "No!" Yes, there are many churches, with many sermons, prayers, and songs, but most of them are geared toward adults. Unfortunately, church is not often a place where urban young people can hear a word from God packaged specifically for them.

Many sermons within the urban church speak to the conditions, felt needs, and issues of urban adults. They are not contextualized to urban youth issues, which are very different. Is it any surprise that in most urban churches young people sit in the back or in the balcony, fall asleep, write notes, or sneak outside when they do come? This is why urban youth ministry must move more and more toward becoming a profession, and why developing more urban youth communication tools and resources is absolutely essential!

Speak the Words of God

Urban youth need a radical alternative to the words of the world. Too many hear only words of destruction, anger, pain, and hopelessness. They hear far too much about how they're just like their no-good father or mother, about how bad they are and that they will never amount to anything.

Who will speak words from God to them? Most urban young people don't hear much about how God loves them, how God cares for them, and how he can relate to the daily issues, challenges, and barriers they face. They don't hear that they are valuable, gifted, and talented, and that God has a wonderful plan for their lives. They've never been told they're not too young to have an impact in the world.

Jesus spoke words of life, not death, when he encountered a woman caught in adultery, a man with a legion of demons, and a woman with an issue of blood. He saw and spoke differently to those others had left for dead. This way of communicating is critical, especially in dealing with at-risk youth.

When I go into juvenile detention centers, I try to remember that I am a representative of a God with the ability to speak to those left for dead. I've looked at urban young men through a cell door and told them that God created them to be kings, not criminals. They've already been told how bad they are and what they really deserve based on what they've done and that they'll never amount to anything. So I tell them they are valuable and special and that the mistakes they've made can never change the fact that before they were formed in the womb, God had a plan for their lives. I tell them they are men of destiny, if only they would stop running from God's plan for their lives.

Earn the Right to Be Heard

Once we're convinced just how relevant the Bible is to the issues of urban youth, we must focus on earning the right to proclaim it to them.

Hip-hop artists, whether you like them or not, have earned the right to be heard by urban youth. Why? They're marketed as being a part of the subculture, the world in which urban youth live—whether they actually come from the 'hood or not. This principle is what the gospel of Jesus Christ is all about. God became flesh and entered the world of humanity.

Earning the right to speak the words of God into the lives of urban young people requires us to be willing to enter into their world. We must get out of our "church" world and enter the world of young people. Jesus understood this when he went to Samaria and met the woman at the well. The Bible says in John 4 that Jesus "had to" go into Samaria. Why?

Even though the religious people ignored Samaria, Jesus could not. He had a sense of urgency to reach this subculture that was despised by the dominant Jewish culture. He wasn't waiting for the Samaritans to come to him. He went into their world! And the result was one of the most fruitful encounters of Jesus' earthly ministry. Just as Jesus had to go to Samaria, we have to go into the world of urban youth. Staying in the church or some other safe religious place has never shown itself effective when it comes to reaching urban young people.

One way to win the right to be heard is by asking questions. In doing so we learn about the joys, pain, fears, dreams, and feelings of urban young people. When Jesus met the woman at the well he began his conversation by asking for a drink of water. Too many people speak to urban youth before they really understand them and consequently miss the mark. Pastors often preach over the heads and under the hearts of urban young people because they haven't taken the time to really listen to their felt needs.

Enter Their World

I'm the girls' varsity head basketball coach at Patrick Henry High School. This is the vehicle God opened up for me to be able to get into the world of urban young people in the city of Minneapolis. There are many urban youth whose lives I would never have had the opportunity to speak into if I had waited for them to come to my youth group.

As an example, last year when the girls were getting ready to play our top rival team, I could hear them from my office around the corner from the locker room. They were playing rap music loudly on a boom box. That didn't bother me, as I like rap and hip-hop music. What did bother me was that the rapper kept using the "b" word. Over and over he repeated it. I asked my assistant to go in there and tell the girls to turn it off. I was so angry that I went upstairs to the gym to clear my head a bit.

As I headed back downstairs I met the girls at the top of the stairs. Before I could think, I yelled at them, "You are not b——-s! You are queens and women of destiny. I never want to hear you refer to yourselves in that way again!"

My eyes were close to tears and I was shaking. After the game Chauntel came into my office crying. I thought she was crying because we lost the game, but she said, "I just wanted to say thank you. No one ever called me a queen before." It was then I realized why I coach girls' basketball. God wants to let inner-city girls know they are queens! This would never have happened had I chosen to stay in the comfort zone of my church.

Use Stories

Share your stories. Remember that you were once a teenager yourself. You don't need to be an eloquent orator to communicate effectively to urban youth. They're not looking for eloquent preachers or teachers, but for people who will be real with them. And what they need are stories that speak directly to the issues they're dealing with.

When we stand before young people and tell them to stay virgins until they're married, they are saying to themselves, "Well, were you a virgin when you got married?" Be honest with them about how it was for you. Share the pains of not following Christ as well as how God has rewarded your obedience to his ways. When I speak to urban youth I share stories about how I was as a teenager as well as stories about my life now. When you set the example of being real, you allow the youth to let their guard down and be honest too.

I tell young people that they are gifted and valuable, and then I tell them how I didn't see myself that way when I was growing up. I spent most of my teenage years wishing I was someone else. As you share your life, you help them reflect on their own lives more honestly. This is why hip-hop artists have had such an influence on urban youth. They're "street storytellers." As they share their stories, young people are drawn in and begin to see connection, relevance, and even application to their own lives.

Effective storytelling has always been a transformational force in urban communities. The Civil Rights movement was spawned with stories of hope, freedom, and liberation. We, as communicators of the gospel, must reclaim our rightful place as storytellers of transformation to today's urban youth culture!

Effective storytelling goes way beyond words, though. If you are married with children, for example, you can communicate Christian truths just by inviting a young person to your home for dinner. Doing so allows them to see firsthand what a Christian family looks like. Your family doesn't have to be perfect; you just need to be real and allow the love of Christ to shine through you. The Apostle Paul described this well in 1 Thessalonians 2:8: "We loved you so much that we were delighted to share with you not only the gospel of

God but our lives as well, because you had become so dear to us."

When Jesus walked the earth, he had a far greater influence upon young people than hip-hop artists do today. Consider how many people were drawn to him—there were so many that the disciples had to try to keep them away. And most of those who came felt like outcasts in mainstream society. I believe if Jesus Christ walked the streets today, urban youth would be drawn to him. He would communicate to them not only through his words, but through his actions as well. We are the voice, hands, and feet of Jesus.

God has a word for urban young people. We must see ourselves as ambassadors of that word—willing to speak words and live lifestyles in front of them that will point them to the love, grace, transformation, and challenge of the Christian life.

Endnotes

[1] The Associated Press, "State's Minority Population Rises Sharply," WCCO News, http://www.channel4000.com (December 19, 1997).

[2] Lourdes Medrano Leslie, "Minnesota's Hmong Double in a Decade," *Minneapolis Star Tribune* (August 1, 2001), http://www.startribune.com.

Chapter 3 The Code of the Streets

Dean Borgman

G od loves the city. He tells us so in passages like Jeremiah 29:4-7; Jonah 4:11; Matthew 23:37; and Revelation 21:2. Over the years I've had the privilege of meeting many, many youth workers who are beacon lights on dark city streets. Bringing light into the darkness of today's inner-city neighborhoods and the pervasive street culture within them is difficult work. So I salute those who have been there for kids and tried to make a difference in urban neighborhoods, and I hope you will be encouraged as you read this chapter.

Defining the Terms

Effecting change in any existing situation first requires a basic understanding of that situation. So let's begin by defining some terms.

Urbanization describes the global movement from rural and traditional cultures to life in the city. Today, the majority of those in America and much of the world are urban dwellers. In addition, we depend on many technologies and buy, rather than raise, our own food. Even more specific to this book, we define *urbanites* as those people groups who live in cities such as Los Angeles, New York, Chicago, or Atlanta—as opposed to those who live outside the city limits as suburbanites.

Urban youth work might include ministry to a wide variety of young people who reside in metropolitan areas, but in this book we are not talking about interacting with those middle- and upper-class professionals and their families who live within the city limits. For our purposes, we will define urban youth work as reaching out to the urban poor of disadvantaged inner-city neighborhoods. These neighborhoods, and those who live in them, are very much alive, though they struggle mightily against the consequences of personal and environmental poverty and neglect.

Understanding the Issues

Ministering effectively to today's urban youth is a very complex undertaking. I have been an avid student of urban youth culture for more than fifty years, since beginning as a youth worker in Connecticut in the 1950s, then working on the streets of Harlem and Manhattan's Lower East Side in the turbulent 1960s, up through my present role as a professor of urban youth ministry. The basic needs are the same, but the issues have changed dramatically.

Poverty

According to sociologist Elijah Anderson, many of the problems besetting the poor inner-city black community (although his comments apply equally to other racial minority groups) stem from the violence that rises out of the circumstances of the ghetto poor: the lack of jobs that pay a living wage; limited basic public services such as police response, building maintenance, trash pickup, adequate lighting; the stigma of race; drug use and drug trafficking; alienation; and lack of hope for the future.[1]

One 13-year-old Chicago teenager describes his housing-project neighborhood this way:

"Our neighborhood is a fun neighborhood if you know what you're doing. If you act like a little kid in this neighborhood, you're not gonna last too long. 'Cause if you play childish games in the ghetto, you're gonna find a childish bullet in your childish brain."[2]

He goes on to talk about living in a war zone, knowing two friends who were shot and killed in a week when he was just eight years old, hearing gunfire on a regular basis, walking down streets of abandoned buildings, seeing kids doing mostly nothing, passing bums on the street, and stepping over garbage while reading graffiti.[3]

Another urban teenager describes growing up in a Boston inner-city neighborhood quite differently:

"My neighborhood might have drugs and violence, but I guarantee, if there were just some more jobs, there would be less drugs being sold. If there were more clubs, there wouldn't be so much hanging out on the street and violence."[4]

While these two descriptions might sound contradictory, both perspectives are true.

Street Culture

French anthropologist Philippe Bourgois has studied the culture that emerges from poor communities in general, and racially concentrated areas in particular. He says that the physical poverty many urban youth grow up in, compounded by racial and cultural divides, has spawned an inner-city street culture. This culture is made up of a complex and often-conflicting web of beliefs, symbols, modes of interaction, values, and ideologies that have emerged in opposition to exclusion from mainstream society.[5]

In my classes over the years, many middle-class, suburban students have been surprised and even have argued with me when I've stated that the majority of residents in the ghetto are good, hardworking people with middle-class values. Yet there is a mindset held by a distinct minority of urban dwellers that is at work on the streets and whose power dictates much of what happens in the neighborhood.

Many who reside in the most economically depressed, drug- and crime-ridden pockets of the city subconsciously move to the beat of a "code of the street." At the heart of this code is a set of informal behavioral rules organized around a desperate search for respect. Possessing respect (or "juice") is highly valued for its ability to shield the ordinary person from interpersonal violence on the street.[6]

According to Philippe Bourgois, "Street culture offers an alternative forum for autonomous personal dignity" for those to whom such dignity is otherwise out of reach. "This 'street culture of resistance' is not a coherent, conscious universe of political opposition but, rather, a spontaneous set of rebellious practices that in the long term have emerged as an oppositional style."[7]

The streets retain an amazing power of family, education, employment, and social life all combined in one. The power of the street sometimes seems to have even a spiritual quality. You see boys and girls leaving their traditional families to form more meaningful relationships on the streets. As they drop out of school and become caught up in the economy of the streets, the streets become their principal educational institution, source of sustenance, and place of connection and belonging.

The Street Economy

Realistically, the economics of the city should not work. Few, if any, available jobs can cover the high cost of urban rent, food, medicines, clothes, travel, and other necessities. Ghetto economics revolve around complex relationships between low-paying jobs; welfare and other forms of financial assistance to families; and the underground or folk economy, consisting in barter (exchanged services) and illegal occupations, especially drug trade.

Anthropologist Philippe Bourgois explains how this underground economy allows people in neighborhoods like East Harlem to afford some amenities that people living in the United States usually consider to be basic necessities. They make a living by repairing cars, doing a construction job here and there, running numbers, or selling drugs.[8]

The power of drugs in urban neighborhoods has been documented in a book (and a documentary aired by MTV) called *The Corner: A Year in the Life of an Inner-City Neighborhood* (1997). Describing one Baltimore neighborhood, it reveals society's failure to understand and reverse the destructive power of addiction and the drug business:

"We need to start over, to admit that somehow the forces of history and race, economic theory and human weakness have conspired to create a new and peculiar universe in our largest cities."[9]

Kids who have succumbed to this oppositional street culture to escape the pressures of the streets find that they are no freer from stress. Many live with continual concerns about getting high and getting money. Additionally, there may be threats from other gangs or random mayhem. Each person must assess how much "juice" he or she carries out into the streets.

It's not safe to venture into the 'hood with uncool fashions, and yet to be fashionable and sport the hottest jacket or shoes or gold is to put one's life on the line. Many feel as if life is just one big game of Russian roulette. They don't expect to live past their early twenties, and if they do, it probably will be only because they have landed long prison sentences.

Identity

An inner-city child grows up, like all children, needing love, a sense of worth from achievements, and community. A child also needs to grow toward healthy manhood or womanhood. Imagine a lobster unable to shed its shell. The flesh within still keeps growing. But if the shell will not release, that flesh will turn to tough, abnormal fiber. Likewise, when social pressures impede human growth, a toughness often develops as antisocial manhood or womanhood emerges.

Identity is a primary issue for teenagers everywhere. Society can produce conditions under which it is very difficult to clarify one's identity, especially for many of our urban minority students, who struggle between identifying with American culture and the traditions of their heritage.

I've already touched on the issue of respect, but its importance is also closely tied to identity. In suburban shootings and urban violence, we see what happens when young people, especially boys, are denied respect. They understand respect as the foundation of all ethical behavior. Youth leaders would be wise to realize that all discipline is based on one word: respect. Society and peers have cruelly wrung respect out of many young people these days. Be mindful of the role God would have you play in its restoration. It is the basis of all our relationships and communication.

Failing Social Systems

Five social systems are of primary importance in shaping children growing up these days: family, community, schools, media, and peers. Children are receiving less from families, communities, and school systems because these systems are under enormous stress themselves. The general dysfunction of our society is passed on to families who, in turn, socialize children in dysfunctional ways. It is critical that urban youth workers pay attention to families and how they can minister to them, rather than try to ignore or take the place of them. Likewise, we must invest in our communities, and not limit that investment only to churches. To ignore our inner-city communities is to abandon our children.

Schools are our third primary social system. To understand what inner-city schools can do to children, begin with Jonathan Kozol's *Death at an Early Age* (East Rutherford, NJ: Dutton/Plume, 1969, 1990). The mere title of this book provides a handle for what we see on the faces of the city's "little people." The intellectual light in the eyes of many urban children begins to dim around third grade. Sadly, much of inner-city education makes students feel dumber by the year.

As families', communities', and schools' effectiveness diminishes, two other social systems increase in influence—the role of the media and the effect of peer pressure. Not enough has been written about the influence of media on inner-city children. Urban youth ministers must be ardent students of the media and its influence upon their young people. A balanced critique of rap music and a study of the effects of consumerism on black, urban children are good starting points. Check out books like these: Adam Sexton, ed.,

Rap On Rap: Straight Up Talk on Hip-Hop Culture (New York, NY: Delta, 1995); Bakari Kitwana, *The Rap on Gangsta Rap* (Chicago, IL: Third World Press, 1994); and Elizabeth Chin, *Purchasing Power: Black Kids and American Consumer Culture* (Minneapolis, MN: University of Minnesota Press, 2001).

Finally, there is the influence of peers on inner-city kids. First consider the need for, and positive power of, friendships. All teenagers must work out their identity with feedback from peers. Friends support the difficult transition from family to independence.

On the negative side, we know friends can also encourage participation in drinking and chemical highs, promiscuous sexual activity, or gang involvement. It's also true that "decent kids" who are studying hard to make something of their lives sometimes run into discouragement and harassment from peers. I recall one black student, who turned down a basketball game to study, being told by his friend, "Uh-oh, sellout time...I just don't want you getting caught up in all that white man's knowledge, or whatnot."

Ministering within the "culture of the streets" is as challenging as any foreign mission field in the world. Christian urban youth workers must be many things for these young people: friends, social workers, missionaries, pastors, and more. The challenges are unending, but so is the potential fruit for those who are called and labor in the power of the Holy Spirit. Hang in there, and keep praying, "Thy Kingdom come. Thy will be done on earth as it is in heaven!"

Endnotes

[1] Elijah Anderson, *Code of the Street* (New York, NY: W.W. Norton & Co., 1999), 32.

[2] LeAlan Jones and Lloyd Newman with David Isay, *Our America: Life and Death on the South Side of Chicago* (New York, NY: Scribner, 1997), 33.

[3] Jones and Newman, *Our America*, 33-36.

[4] Vernice Smith (16, of West Roxbury High School), "My good 'hood," in The Boston Globe Magazine's "In Our Own Words: Special Issue by and about Urban Youth," February 6, 1994, 18.

[5] Philippe Bourgois, *In Search of Respect: Selling Crack in El Barrio* (New York, NY: Cambridge Univ. Press, 1995), 8.

[6] Elijah Anderson, *Code of the Street*, 9-10.

[7] Philippe Bourgois, *In Search of Respect*, 8.

[8] Philippe Bourgois, *In Search of Respect*, 3.

[9] David Simon and Edward Burns, *The Corner: A Year in the Life of an Inner-City Neighborhood* (New York, NY: Broadway Books, 1997), 60.

Chapter 4
Creating Youth Ministry That Crosses Cultures

Joel Van Dyke

I grew up in a homogenous Midwest community where everyone had blonde hair and blue eyes like myself. It was not until I played high school varsity baseball that I became acquainted with African-American, Latino, American Indian, and Asian teenagers; and I never developed any significant cross-cultural friendships until well into college.

My journey into urban cross-cultural ministry began during my third year of college when I moved to Chicago to pursue psychological research experience that I hoped would help me get accepted into a Ph.D. program in clinical psychology. For the first time in my life I was the one who was different from everybody else. I became incredibly passionate about urban cross-cultural ministries during my senior year of college while I was working with gang kids and helping plant a church in South Chicago. It was there that I also received my call to ministry.

After a year or so of trying to work out my calling in the inner city of Chicago, I was able to dedicate an entire summer to full-time missions work with children and youth in North Philadelphia. Near the end of that summer, I had my first of several life-changing, cross-cultural experiences.

One hot summer afternoon, Yung, a seven-year-old Korean boy, had come over to the house where I was staying with other missionaries to show me his new bike. With him was eight-year-old Luis, a kid who had been part of our day camp.

After watching them perform a few wheelies, I went into the kitchen to get them some iced tea. Suddenly Luis burst in screaming that a teenager had taken off with Yung's bike. I arrived outside just in time to see Yung picking himself up off the asphalt and a teenager peddling around the corner with Yung's new bike.

I was furious and ran as fast as I could, hoping to catch the thief and return the bike, but I returned empty-handed. Tears were pouring down Yung's face. I had no idea what to do or say. Suddenly Luis had an idea.

"Hey, can you pray for Yung's bike?"

"Sure," I said. "Let's pray for Yung's bike right now."

I grabbed their hands and began praying. When I finished I expected them to take turns praying as well. When I heard nothing, I opened my eyes only to find them staring at me. I asked why they hadn't prayed for the bike, too, especially since it was Luis' idea. That's when Luis said, "I thought only white people could pray."

I was stunned. Suddenly I realized that much of what I had been doing and saying in that community had caused people to see me in the place of Jesus. That evening I got down on my knees and asked God to reveal to me the errors of my ways that would lead such a precious little boy to conclude that "only white people could pray."

Cross-Cultural Ministry in the Bible

In the weeks, months, and years that followed, I began to read my Bible in a totally different way. In it I saw both positive and negative models for cross-cultural ministry. For instance, the woman from Samaria and all of her neighbors were recipients of Jesus' cross-cultural ministry as recorded in John 4. Acts 10 tells us about some of the lessons Peter had to learn regarding associating with Gentiles.

Daniel had a bilingual, bicultural ministry in the seat of Babylon. He was brought to a secular position of power, yet even with all the cultural challenges around him he never compromised his integrity. Jonah ran away from a cross-cultural challenge because of his hatred for a foreign people he did not want to see receive God's mercy.

Ruth is a great example of a cross-cultural pilgrim whose decision to leave her homeland and follow the God of Naomi was honorable to God. To her hapless mother-in-law she said, "Where you go I will go...Your people will be my people and your God my God. Where you die I will die, and there I will be buried" (Ruth 1:16b-17a).

The story of two disciples on the Emmaus road in Luke 24 is a wonderful model for cross-cultural ministry. Jesus encountered these men as they were heading back home in discouragement because, as they explained to Jesus, they had hoped that Jesus "was the one who was going to redeem Israel" (Luke 24:21a).

Jesus' response was brilliant. He asked them questions and listened intently to their story as he walked along with them. Only after he had traveled with them for some time did he begin to break down what the Scriptures say concerning himself. As they approached their town, they invited Jesus into their home. He accepted their invitation and once inside at the table, "he took bread, gave thanks, broke it and began to give it to them." It was then that "their eyes were opened" (Luke 24:30-31).

What so often happens in cross-cultural urban settings is that, in our zeal, we begin proclaiming something before we have earned the right to do so. We force ourselves as hosts of the good news before earning the right into people's lives as guests. We haven't walked with them, talked to them, or listened to their stories.

The gospel is not advice; it is news. Advice patronizes; good news liberates. Jesus proclaimed the good news of the gospel, but only after he had walked and talked with people. Jesus earned the right to be invited into their homes by the way he approached and responded to them.

With these thoughts as a backdrop, let me present four guiding principles that I have learned over the past sixteen years of ministering cross-culturally. I must admit that I have learned far more from my blunders than my successes, which makes me grateful for the many young people and their families who have incarnated for me the grace of God by the patience they have returned in the face of my many errors.

Sit at the Feet of Other Cultures

In Luke 10:38-42 we receive rich insight into a cross-cultural ministry principle through the story of Mary and Martha. Martha was scurrying about, making needless preparations for Jesus' time in their home—preparations that apparently were far more important to her than they were to her guest. Martha, out of frustration, snapped at Jesus, asking him to rebuke Mary for her laziness and insensitivity. Jesus gently answered, "Martha, Martha,...you are worried and upset about many things, but only one thing is needed. Mary has chosen what is better, and it will not be taken away from her."

I came to my ministry in North Philadelphia as a Martha. I was trained from childhood to take charge and make things happen wherever I went. My motto for successful living was to generate ideas, mobilize resources, take charge, and stay in control.

I came to Philadelphia in the summer of 1988 with visions and dreams of all the great things I was going to do for God. What I eventually heard from God was that I was worried and upset about many things that were important to *me*, but were of little importance to those whom I had been called to serve. In cross-cultural ministry we must first sit at the feet of the culture as Mary did at the feet of Jesus if we want to be relevant, understanding, and practical with the gospel in context.

How does a person who is ministering cross-culturally go about sitting as opposed to merely doing? This begins with a conscious decision to take on the posture of a student rather than a teacher.

Take on the Posture of a Student

Undoubtedly, you have relevant education under your belt as well as a diverse array of service learning experiences. But you still have to earn the right to "teach" in a cross-cultural setting. That right comes only through the development of trust. And trust happens best from a posture of humility rather than an assumption that we have the "goods" that others need in order to be successful.

Working in the midst of a hip-hop culture, I knew that if I wanted to be relevant, I would need schooling under the tutelage of a master hip-hop craftsman. I invited fourteen-year-old rapper and hip-hop iconoclast Ralfy Rosario out for a Coke and fries one day after school and commenced my education. Armed with a pen and notebook, I drilled him with questions for a couple of hours about hip-hop gear, slang, rappers, and so on. I left with several pages of notes, a wealth of firsthand knowledge, and most importantly the respect of an influential fourteen-year-old.

Shortly after my first class with Ralfy, he started to become much more interested in what I had to share about the Word of God. That first meeting began a strong, mutually beneficial relationship that remains strong to this day. And Ralfy is now in full-time ministry at our church, heading up Asaph Studios, our media arts center.

Exegete Your Community

In addition to taking the posture of a student, learning to exegete one's community is essential. To *exegete* is to correctly discern what is really there, as opposed to *isogesis*, which is the adding of things that were never there. Far too often, zealous youth workers attempt to force their culturally influenced understanding of God isogetically into the lives of the kids they're ministering to.

It never ceases to amaze me, when I consult with Anglo urban youth workers, how often retreats out to the "country" become their number one ministry strategy. If that is God's choice dwelling, what does that say to a young person whose world is surrounded by noisy streets and stagnant water? Do they have to leave their world to find God, who is out chillin' in the country?

One of my ministry heroes is Juan Flores, the pastor of a little church in Chicago's gang-infested West Side. During a visit to a little "cabin" that he built adjacent to a back alley behind his church, he boldly stated, "I'm tired of people always telling my kids that they have to go out to the country to find God. That's the reason that I built this little 'retreat center' right here in the city. I want my kids to learn that retreating with Jesus is a daily spiritual exercise, not a weekend trip."

Some of my most profound spiritual insights and encounters with God have come as I have learned to recognize how Christ is alive and well in the world in which the kids I have been called to love, live. A few years back a young man shared with me an entry in his journal. He had written about seeing an example of God's love in the form of an open fire hydrant on a hot summer day. I have never looked the same since at kids playing in the spray of a fire hydrant.

God is everywhere in my neighborhood, and the discipline of carefully exegeting the neighborhood around me helps me grow in Christ and makes the message of his love alive and relevant for those who live here with me.

Pursue Cross-Cultural Mentors

Another important discipline for ministering cross-culturally is to pursue personal and ministry mentors of the culture around you. I meet regularly with a couple of Latino and African-American pastors whom I uphold as ministry and spiritual fathers. Over the past twelve years they have taught me more about the life, love, and sacrifice of ministry in the inner city than a lifetime of seminary classes ever could. Most of what I know or have accomplished in urban ministry is credited to what God has done in my life through these mentoring relationships.

When it comes to deep relationships of love and accountability, we tend to stay close to those who are just like us and then wonder why it is so frustrating to try to understand the way those "other people" think and act.

There are three pitfalls we are in danger of falling into when these principles are ignored:

1. The Ignorance Pitfall. Early on in my ministry I had to undo a serious mistake made by a well-intentioned but woefully ignorant youth worker I supervised.

A young lady from a Central American family, whose parents had immigrated before their daughter was born, was struggling over her relationship with a young man that her parents disapproved of. The youth worker, himself an immigrant to Philadelphia from the "country" of California, had a "great" idea for easing her parents' concern over this young man whom he knew to be a very upstanding, committed Christian.

In the past, this youth worker would often ease parents' concerns over dating by volunteering to go along as a chaperone. Many parents were relieved and appreciative of this youth worker's willingness to give of his time in this way.

Without ever taking the time to get to know the deep tensions experienced between immigrant parents and their kids over "American culture," he invited himself into the family's home and offered his chaperoning services to the parents. The young lady cowered in disbelief that her youth worker would condone a relationship she knew her parents strictly forbade at her age. As a result, it was three months before she was even allowed by her parents to come to our youth center again, and that was only after significant intervention and apologies from our youth ministry team.

2. The Paternalistic Pitfall. Many enter urban youth ministry determined to win the city for God. But they often forget to include God in the process. They know what "those kids" need and believe they have what it takes to make it happen. But God isn't so interested in our agendas; he's working out his plan already in a myriad of ways through many people.

In 2 Kings 6, Elisha's servant was overwhelmed at the sight of the Aramean forces with their horses and chariots. He cried out to Elisha in desperation. But Elisha didn't pray for God to show up on the scene. Instead, he prayed that his distracted servant would have the eyes to see the presence and plan of God, who was already on the scene, as manifested through an army of horses and chariots of fire.

Sitting at the feet of another's culture helps us to develop 20/20 spiritual vision in seeing God's plan for his people and joining it, as opposed to developing one of our own.

3. The Power Pitfall. This final pitfall is perhaps most dangerous of all. Those of us who are working cross-culturally in the city must learn to give up control. When John the Baptist was confronted with the fact that his followers had abandoned him to follow this new teacher named Jesus, he stated, "That joy is mine, and it is now complete. He must become greater; I must become less" (John 3:29b-30).

Sitting at the feet of another culture means just that—sitting. It means loving, serving, and striving to become less so that others, through Christ, can become more. Show me an urban youth worker who is on a power trip, and I'll show you someone who needs to spend some significant time sitting at the feet of the culture he or she has been called to serve.

Celebrate Differences

The second major principle of building a ministry that crosses cultures is to learn to celebrate differences. Far too often we look at differences with suspicion and distrust, rather than embracing and celebrating them. As I consult with ministries around my city, I think this is one of the areas we are failing most miserably in.

When I first started working for the Philadelphia Project for Youth Ministry, one of my responsibilities was to head up a citywide student leadership program. There were thirty-three participating churches throughout the city from sixteen different denominations. The ethnic makeup was equally diverse.

We began the year with a retreat, followed by bimonthly training events. By midyear, the enthusiasm and participation were severely waning, and relationships between student leaders remained far more superficial than we had hoped by this time.

It was then that we decided to host a multi-ethnic praise and worship celebration. We asked each group to participate by showing the others how they worshipped in their own tradition. A group of teenagers from a Spanish-speaking Pentecostal church opened the evening by leading everyone in traditional *coritos*. Then the Cambodian youth taught us how to sing a popular praise song in their native tongue and with traditional instruments. The Chinese students did the same in Mandarin. The Messianic Congregation shared a song in Hebrew and dressed it up with some Davidic praise dancers.

We also had some rappers, a poem, a contemporary gospel group and a twenty-member traditional gospel choir. The evening culminated with the sounds of shouting and drums led by a forty-member drill team. This celebration of diversity did wonders to create unity within that group of thirty churches, and the rest of our events that year were profoundly more effective. And the praise gathering became an annual event!

Although such events would be nearly impossible to replicate on an individual church level, the principle remains the same. Differences in your youth group and the surrounding community need to be identified, affirmed, and celebrated. While this may sound very basic, few urban youth ministries do anything proactive to engage diverse cultures, even though they are surrounded by them. In the apostle Paul's analogy of the human body as an illustration of the spiritual body of Christ in 1 Corinthians 12 and Romans 12, he expressly states that the parts of the body "belong" to one another and have need for one another. Urban youth workers are successful cross-culturally when they understand and live out the "belongingness" and "needfulness" that make up the body of Christ.

When this celebration-of-differences principle is neglected, there are two common pitfalls urban youth workers are in danger of falling into:

1. The Stereotyping Pitfall. Failing to sit at the feet of other cultures causes us to be woefully ignorant about their culture and makes us prone to believing and perpetuating false stereotypes. When my brother-in-law teaches urban youth culture classes at our local Bible college, he loves to introduce himself by saying, "Hi, my name is Ruben Ortiz. Yes, I am Puerto Rican, but I do not steal hubcaps or graffiti walls." His point is obvious: Don't make assumptions about me based simply on stereotypes.

2. The Impersonating Pitfall. Youth workers slide into this pitfall when their attempts to "fit in" or "be accepted" overshadow the unique cultural traits they themselves bring to the ministry. This pitfall is especially luring for young urban youth workers who think that to successfully reach kids they need to "be down" by "sportin' the right gear" and "spittin' the right slang." But kids in the city can spot an impersonator a mile away, and nothing turns them off quicker.

When I first started out as a youth pastor in an almost exclusively Latino youth group, I thought I had to set aside my Midwestern upbringing and become like the kids around me. I started wearing their clothes, using their slang, and even listening to their music. I soon discovered the fallacy of my actions. Kids in the city respond to genuineness and integrity. Be yourself and celebrate your own cultural uniqueness as well as the culture of those around you.

Build Bridges

The third principle for successful cross-cultural ministry is to learn to build bridges. This principle springs forth from the notion that for cross-cultural ministry relationships to be successful there must be give and take on both sides. The bridge we're attempting to build is not a one-way bridge; it goes both ways.

Christian leaders in general, and youth workers in particular, are notorious for getting into "one-way" relationships where they resist showing any signs of vulnerability for fear that they will be seen as weak. I have met many who have moved into a community from elsewhere because they have something to "give." Their motives are great but their relationships tend to become one-way as opposed to reciprocal.

Church-planting strategies—where groups of people move into cross-cultural communities together at the same time—can also have an unintended negative impact. While such a strategy might be a good way to build up a quick critical mass of people, it works against the principle of bridge building because it communicates the perception that there is no need for others from the local community. "What we want from you is your attendance at what we're doing so that we can be successful in what we've set out to do," is the message that's often communicated.

When I became a homeowner in North Philly, I lacked the handyman skills necessary to renovate a city row house. I had no good tools, no firsthand knowledge, and no spare time to attend Home Depot workshops. Before I had such needs, my relationships with the families of the youth I ministered to were very superficial, limited to getting them to sign permission forms for trips and exchanging quick hellos while I was picking up or dropping off their children from youth events.

But when I was confronted with plumbing needs, electrical problems, and carpentry projects, suddenly I found myself spending five or six hours on a Saturday with a father of one of my teenagers as he shared with me his skills, resources, and experience. It was through such experiences that many of those relationships with parents were deepened.

A devastating pitfall awaits those youth workers who neglect to follow this principle of cultural bridge-building.

The Project Pitfall

I learned about this pitfall the hard way when 21-year-old Juan had the courage to confront me with his pain and hurt over lunch one day. He had grown up on one of the most notorious drug trafficking streets in North Philly and worked there himself selling drugs for a couple of years.

Juan dedicated his life to Christ after several of his friends had been killed as a result of their lifestyle choices. Soon he became very passionate about learning all he could about his new life in Christ. He was a joy to spend time with, and his hunger for the Word was a magnet for many of our willing mentors. Juan was the kind of youth that urban youth workers love to have on their résumé of successes. He became almost a poster boy for the success of our youth ministry.

During our lunch, Juan seemed uncharacteristically anxious, as though he was struggling to say something he had been pondering for quite some time.

"Pastor Joel," he finally said, "this is hard for me to say, but it's been really bothering me. It's almost as though for the past five or six years of my time in youth ministry I've been more like a project to you and the others than a person."

I was stunned. And while I had never thought about this before, I knew he was absolutely right. I am indebted to Juan for his honesty because ever since, I have used his comments as a litmus test to evaluate my successful adaptation of the bridge-building principle of effective cross-cultural ministry.

Have Incarnational Presence

The theology of the Incarnation is an integral truth of orthodox Christianity as depicted in the verse, "The Word became flesh and made his dwelling among us" (John 1:14). Incarnational presence as a missiological principle is just as integral for effectiveness in cross-cultural ministry.

A woman came to a friend of mine a few years ago. She could not understand why she wasn't connecting with the youth in the urban community she felt called to.

"Where do you live?" asked this veteran youth pastor.

"I live in the suburbs," she responded.

When he asked why, she said, "I am here to do ministry with kids, not to get shot for them."

To that he responded, "Well, that's your problem. For those of us who have grown up and live in this neighborhood, a basic ingredient for trust is whether or not we can trust someone to watch our back. I don't mean to be rude, but if you aren't willing to take a bullet for the kids in my neighborhood, you have no business trying to befriend them."

As hard as those words are to hear, they lie at the foundation of what it means to minister incarnationally with urban young people. It is the price to pay for a youth worker who desires to build a ministry that crosses culture and has an incarnational presence in the lives of urban young people. To be involved in any significant outreach in any neighborhood demands that we call it home. When there is a fire, a shooting, a trash problem, or drug dealing in a neighborhood, it's not paid community organizers who will address the issues; those who are most directly affected by the problems will solve them.

I realized this firsthand the day I was threatened by a raging drunk in front of my house as he accused me of looking at him the wrong way. As this man, nearly twice my size, screamed vulgarities at me and bumped up against my chest with his fists clenched, I was suddenly pushed away from him as someone stepped in behind me.

It was Felix, a senior from my youth group who was also a boxer. Accompanying him were two other kids from our youth group who were not happy with the way this man was treating me. Felix told him that if he wanted to mess with his youth pastor he would have to get through him and his two friends first. Uttering a few more obscenities, he crawled back into his car and sped away.

"You okay, Pastor Joel?" Felix asked. "Nobody messes with my pastor without going through me first." I learned firsthand what it meant for someone to have "my back." Oh, how I pray I will be found faithful to do the same when the tables are turned.

I believe these four issues of cross-cultural effectiveness that I have covered in this chapter are absolutely essential in the rapidly urbanizing and multicultural world in which we now live. When God gave us the great commission to go make disciples of all nations, either we went out too slowly or simply failed. But it seems God isn't waiting for us anymore. He's bringing the nations to our cities and putting them at our doorsteps. We must be ready to respond to the task before us, trusting that we are the ones God wants to use to incarnate the good news of his Son, Jesus Christ!

Chapter 5
Ministering to African-American Youth and Families

Rudy Howard

I f your calling may lead you or has led you to ministering with urban African-American youth, congratulations! Today's urban African-American youth are leading the way with a paradigm shift for living in and for the city. This paradigm shift affects the way urban black youth and families think, feel, and act, and what they will respond to.

As a fifty-two-year-old black baby boomer born and raised in Chicago, I've spent the last thirty years in ministry to black urban youth. I'd like to share my perspective on some of the unique social, racial, spiritual, and psychological issues facing today's urban African-American families and an offshoot—hip-hop youth culture.

Save the Children

A few years ago, while listening to a taped message from a conference, calling for the need to "save the children," Carl and Sandra felt a personal sense of urgency as lay youth leaders to respond to the call to serve African-American urban youth and families. The trouble was, the tape had been recorded thirty years earlier!

You see, "save the children" is still the cry in our African-American urban metro areas. Although deeply concerned about this special collection of God's people, Carl and Sandra felt inadequate to meet their needs. They were also confronted with the fact that they were not in touch with the youth culture.

Soon they were wondering, "Who's included in this mission field, and what is this hip-hop youth culture anyway?"

Background

Though statistics lack a human face, they convey certain realities. Black children are more likely than white children to suffer many of life's hardships such as being born to a teenager or single mother, experiencing poverty, living in a female-headed family, or being murdered. These facts mean black teenagers start life in a state of oppression just by being born into a black community in America.

As a very general observation, many of today's African-American youth are stereotyped as high- and low-achievers, at risk, high risk, wannabes, hard-core school kids, street kids, good kids, and—worst of all—bad kids.

Oppressed and Possessed

Many of today's black youth are oppressed by the false hope and fantasy that it is possible to attain instant success. In reaction to being locked out of that success through a lack of opportunity or education, or because of racism, many engage in the violence of street gangs and drug and alcohol abuse. They appear to have no vision for tomorrow because, for them, there may be no tomorrow.

In addition, because many black young people come from single-parent families, many are possessed by the fear that they will wake up one morning and be alone. One young lady told me she was continually afraid that one day she would come home and her mom would be gone. This fear of being left alone can be very intense.

Feelings of self-doubt, emotional vulnerability, and a deep sense of inferiority further possess black teenagers and keep them in bondage. While the same can be said for teenagers of any race, such issues run more deeply among blacks, given their historical background.

What, if anything, can be done about the situation of black teenagers being possessed and oppressed?

The Evolution of the Civil Rights Movement

First of all, we of the black middle class must remember from whence we came. We who have lived through and experienced the evolution of the Civil

Rights movement must understand: We are the children of the "promised land."

African Americans born in the 1950s and earlier were born into the pre-civil rights era, a time when there was a sense of hope for tomorrow. Equal access to education, housing, and jobs were the keys to sharing in the "American Dream," and hopes ran high that the passage of civil rights legislation in the early 1960s would establish a better way of life for all, especially African Americans, women, and poor people. We as a people would get to the "promised land" that the late Rev. Martin Luther King Jr. spoke of.

Equipped with higher education and better jobs, many African Americans were elevated into the middle class in the 1970s, '80s, and '90s—but not all of them. The Civil Rights movement helped those groups of blacks in the upper, middle, military, and working classes. But the street and lower classes remain as they were twenty years ago—locked out. Not that every inner-city black family is in the lower class. I would, in fact, say that urban African-American families would fall into three different categories of people—all of whom we are called to reach out to: the educated establishment group, the working literate group, and the need-for-enlightenment group.

The Educated Establishment Group

The educated establishment group is comprised of those from middle- to upper-income families. They tend to have a working understanding of wealth, the future, and how it can affect their lives. Even though they may live a little better than most black families, they are nonetheless plagued by the impact of society's ills. Yet they sometimes have a sense of hope and belief in God or at least something spiritual.

Example: Dr. Robert Blackstone and his wife, attorney Mary Blackstone, have two children, Justin and Tiffany. They attend St. Mark's African Methodist Episcopal Church. The kids are planning to attend Morehouse and Spellman colleges. Justin, who is in high school, has been seen with "gang kids," a mixed group of young people who are trying to find themselves. Tiffany, who is very fashion conscious, is attracted to "roughneck" guys. Although it appears on the outside as though this family is well off, a closer look reveals that a few problems may be brewing. There is at the core of this family, however, a sense of hope in the future.

The Working Literate Group

The working literate group comprises the heart of most urban areas. They are the working class. They work hard for income today so that they may have something tomorrow. They are goal oriented, yet have a hard time meeting all their goals. They are survivors. They need to see Christ manifested on an ongoing daily basis, or they can quickly lose faith.

Example: Loraine Johnson is a single mom with a son named Shawn, who is thirteen years old. Loraine is a pool secretary for the Wonder Bread Company. They attend Third Street Full Gospel Baptist Church. Shawn is headed for King High School in the fall. He and his mom pray that he will survive the summer, as a local gang is pressuring Shawn. Loraine is hoping to buy a home next year. "Lord, help us to hold out" is her prayer.

The Need-for-Enlightenment Group

The need-for-enlightenment group is the group most often referred to when we speak of urban dwellers. Many live for money and for today with no real hope for a future. Most of the negative aspects of our society are part of their everyday life. There is knowledge of God, but at times it seems that he just doesn't care. Oppressed by systemic racism and sexism, they often live in hopeless, powerless, and controlled environments.

Many of them appear to have no vision of tomorrow. When one has no hope in the future, that is soon reflected in the way one lives. They are oppressed by the false hope and fantasy of attaining instant success in whatever they attempt to do—an "I want it and I want it now" attitude. They react to being locked out of that success by concluding that tomorrow is not available to them, and that conclusion drives many to engage in violence or drug abuse.

Example: Kisha is twenty years old and has three kids: Donte (seven), Romaine (five), and Tia (three). All have different fathers. Raheem is Tia's father and the one Kisha is currently dating. Kisha and Raheem are not married, but they are always together. Kisha works part time and receives aid for the older boys. She is very careful to keep her part-time job hidden from the welfare department. Raheem can't hold a job for any length of time. He says he "slangs" (sells weed) to make ends meet. Madear, Kisha's mother, envisions very little hope for the couple and her grandchildren. Kisha tries not to talk about it or think about it too much.

This need-for-enlightenment group is the primary group I want to focus on in this chapter.

Implications for Today's Urban Youth

Post-Civil Rights Babies

The children of African-American families who were born in the post-Civil Rights era have read and heard of the struggle that African Americans, women, and the poor had, but they didn't experience it personally. Therefore, they have a different perception of life and all that it embodies. As a reaction to being locked out of the new American Dream, they respond with discontentment, disillusionment, and cynicism designed as a system of survival.

Although today's urban African-American youth are the grandchildren of the promised land, they lack understanding of the God who brought them to this land. Part of the reason for this lack of understanding may be due to the failure of the African-American boomer generation to pass on all of the gospel and understanding of God in a clear, acceptable way.

Big Mamaism

"Big Mama" historically has been an African-American family cornerstone. Even if there was a grandfather, it was "Big Mama" (grandmother) who held the family together. Provision, protection, and guidance wrapped in loving, kind, strong words came from her wisdom and age.

By contrast, many urban young people today have a grandmother who is as young as 35. There's something missing—through no fault of the young grandmother, who very often takes on the role of mother to her young grandchildren because of a daughter who is too young and inexperienced to effectively carry out such a role. But the result is, these young grandmothers simply haven't lived long enough or experienced enough to be the stable voices that grandmothers once were. Many, in fact, are still trying to develop their own lives. Thus, the guidance and influence they provide their grandchildren comes more in the form of information, rather than wisdom.

Youth leaders must be mindful of the need for young people to still receive such wisdom. One solution is to cultivate ministry relationships with the elderly in their communities, who can be available to fill such needed roles for today's inner-city children and youth. There is another benefit to having relationships with those affectionately called "Big Mama"—they tend to be great prayer warriors.

Community vs. Autonomy

All teenagers in America have a need to be part of something, to be accepted and liked. Black teenagers are no exception. They want to be a part of a group, but they feel excluded from certain groups and organizations, often on their own high school campuses. As blacks, our inborn African nature makes us want and expect to be part of a community. It's part of our culture and value system.

This is in sharp contrast to the Anglo-American worldview, which values individualism. Many black teenagers in large and small communities in America contend with these two concepts. This struggle is very real and can be extremely exasperating for many black teenagers.

Chest-of-Drawers Philosophy

Many of today's African-American teenagers have developed a dualistic worldview that looks much like a chest of drawers. Each drawer represents an entirely different aspect of their life. One may be relationships, another entertainment, one education, one jobs, and still another spirituality. The African-American tradition says that God is a part of all the drawers. But hip-hoppers today tend to keep the drawers separate and unrelated to one another. That's why one song on a rap CD can be so spiritual and God-exalting, and the next be repulsive and carnal. It's the same with so many of today's teenagers. On one hand, they can say they're completely committed to a girl or boyfriend, but be entertained the next night by illicit sex with a stranger—all with no apparent internal conflict.

Unmet Needs

Psychologists often speak of adolescents as having a set of basic needs. I would add to the list the need for hope. Young people need to visualize pictures of life and hope for the future, with themselves in it. When people don't see themselves in the future, they act very differently.

Outsiders often remark that tough, urban black children don't act like normal children. A thirteen-year-old in any culture will act like a normal thirteen-year-old when allowed to be in "normal, safe conditions." But most young blacks in urban areas today are not living in normal, safe living conditions. While many young people have their heads on straight and are able to function and do well, many more of them are struggling. And when kids' basic emotional needs aren't met, it shouldn't be surprising that they don't respond in "normal" ways.

A Response: The Birth of Hip-Hop

African Americans don't have a true language and culture apart from the American mainstream dominant culture. As a result, throughout modern times we have developed code languages and subcultures like "beep bop" and soul. But by far the strongest and most impacting has been hip-hop.

Hip-hop began in the South Bronx in the mid-1970s. The early pioneers were rappers like Grandmaster Flash and Kool Herc. The four main symbols of early hip-hop culture were graffiti art, break dancing, DJ'ing (cuttin' and scratching), and emceeing (rapping). Hip-hop is now a lifestyle consisting of its own language, hairstyles, dress and fashion, music, and mind-set. It has lasted over twenty years and has become a billion-dollar industry. The baby boomers never thought it would last this long. Why has it?

Hip-hop culture has had the same effect on older African Americans as the hippie counterculture had on older white Americans. Most African-American baby boomers struggle with the hip-hoppers and rappers like Snoop Dogg, Tupac, Lil' Kim, and P. Diddy. Many have forgotten how our parents struggled with the likes of Parliament-Funkadelic, Millie Jackson, and the "godfather of soul," James Brown. Songs like "It's Your Thing," by the Isley Brothers, and "P. Funk (Wants to Get Funked Up)," by the band Parliament-Funkadelic, caused the hair to stand up on the necks of our parents. But what makes the African-American boomer generation most concerned with today's hip-hop music are the overarching themes of hopelessness and fatalism.

A Hip-Hop Generation

The hip-hop generation also seems to have a different understanding of and belief in God. That is to say, God is a part of the hip-hop culture, but not at the core. This makes it difficult for African-American boomers to have patience and tolerance for many of the actions of the hip-hop generation, as most of them have rejected the values of their parents and grandparents.

Rap music and the language it uses to express thoughts and concepts of this new culture is primarily what has defined this hip-hop generation. But other psychosocial and behavioral characteristics of these young people bear mentioning. In general, they are self-centered; they have an imaginary audience (themselves) and are living a personal fable; they are going through physical, emotional, and psychological changes, and they are discovering the opposite sex and themselves.

How do they think? These teenagers tend to think in short, simple terms, sharp and to the point. They think in pictures and in terms of "what's in it for me?" Because of their loss of innocence, there is no imagination. A very common phrase is " I think I can do it, but I don't know if I can."

How do they feel? Teenagers use rap music to express the anger, hurt, pain, and rage that they feel. Many feel they don't have control of their lives, school, families, and future. They have a "paralyzed will," and this paralysis is not all because of peer pressures. They feel hopeless and unsure about what's going on with and around them. They feel injustice very quickly, and demand to be respected.

To be respected, for many of these young people, means, "Recognize me as a person," "Do you see me?" and most of all "Do you like or love me?" The slang phrase in some urban areas is "Do you feel me?" This expresses well what their hearts and subconscious selves are asking.

How do they act? It has been said that young people are all actors who act out what they see. In reality, they may act fearless but are fearful. They act self-centered, but in fact have low self-esteem. While they attempt to act hard-core, profanity has taken the place of slang, to the point where many young people don't even hear or see themselves as being profane. In many urban areas, if young people are using proper language, attending school, and making good grades, they are said to be "acting white." If that is the case, then the opposite is "acting black." This parallel is shocking and painful for many older African Americans to hear.

There Is Hope

At the core of the African-American hip-hop generation are energy, drive, and resilience. They, like those who have gone before them, have a remnant; that is to say God has not forgotten this generation. There are rappers who have expressed desire to seek God and Christ. Master P, a modern-day rapper, recorded a song that asks a simple question: "Is there a heaven for a gangster?"[1] Yes, Christ said to the thief hanging next to him on the cross, "Today you will be with me in paradise" (Luke 23:43). The charge and challenge is how to make the gospel and the good news real to this hip-hop generation.

What will it take to have an effective ministry to African-American youth of the hip-hop culture as well as their families? Let me suggest a few simple skills and functional processes that have worked in the past.

1. Help lay youth leaders see this ministry as a calling, not just a great cause.

Part of that calling demands that they be ardent students of hip-hop culture and other forces that may have an impact on African-American youth and their families. Our ministries must function like 7-Eleven convenience stores—open 24/7—seeing those in the city with the eyes of Christ. Never forget why we were saved! We were saved to serve. And as we do, Acts 1:8 promises, "You shall receive power when the Holy Spirit has come upon you; and you shall be My witnesses both in Jerusalem, and in all Judea and Samaria, and even to the remotest part of the earth " (New American Standard Bible).

2. Contextualize the gospel message.

Make connections to modern-day scenarios for teenagers. For example, "Nicodemus is like a drug dealer who had to come to Jesus at night for fear of what his friends would say." Or "Look at how Jesus responded to LaTisha, the prostitute who others were trying to stone." Use the Gospels in evangelism and the Epistles for discipleship. Focus on who Jesus was—including the fact that he wasn't white.

3. Do discipleship as well as evangelism.

Sometimes discipleship can have the best of intentions but not turn out so well. It must involve more than Bible study, especially when young people may not read very well. We also must be careful that our discipleship groups are not a cloning process or, even worse, a "holy clique." We can send young people out to share about what Christ has done in their lives, but this does not make disciples. It is the responsibility of every mature Christian to be discipling this younger generation.

Of course, discipleship starts with prayer. Ask the Lord to give a clear vision of where he wants a young person to be at certain times in the discipline process. Set realistic, obtainable goals with the young person. Set aside time for rejoicing when goals and levels are reached. And walk with them, don't just talk.

4. Carry realistic expectations.

The art of shepherding and mentoring is not easy or for the faint of heart. Be prepared for heartbreak and joy. Recognize your limitations and be willing to sometimes be inconvenienced. At the same time, remember the words of our Lord: "Surely I am with you always, to the very end of the age" (Matthew

28:20). There is great comfort in knowing that. We are his disciples, and he has made us whom and what he wants us to be. Therefore, we can do all things through him who supplies all our needs!

There are many challenges facing today's African-American youth and families who reside in our inner cities. And many of them have been given a bad rap for a long time. But God has a different plan, and he still has the last word. As we join God in his purposes, and make those purposes known, he will be faithful to use that which may be considered foolish by some, to confound the wise.

Endnote

[1] Master P, "Is There a Heaven 4 a Gangsta?" *Rhyme & Reason* soundtrack (Priority/Buzz Tone, 1997)

Chapter 6
Ministering to Hispanic-American Youth and Families

Rev. Eli V. Hernandez

Hispanic America's influence on today's urban youth culture has exploded in recent years and continues to gain momentum. As a race, Hispanic Americans are the fastest-growing segment of society; according to census figures, up from 9 percent of the country's population in 1990 to 13 percent in 2000, with a 58 percent increase in numbers.[1] If the Lord is leading you to urban youth ministry, Hispanic Americans and their influence on today's youth culture will no doubt be part of the terrain of your mission field.

I am a second-generation Hispanic American, and I have been working with youth of my culture for the past eleven years in Boston, Massachusetts. Let me begin by sharing a bit about myself and my transition from Puerto Rican thug to Christian youth pastor. With that as a backdrop, I'd like to then discuss some of the issues facing today's urban Hispanic-American teenagers and close by offering some practical suggestions for developing a successful youth ministry to them.

Personal Background

I was born in Mayagüez, Puerto Rico, in 1972, the youngest of four children and the only male in my family. My father left us when I was a year old. My mother moved all of us to New York City and raised us there without any education, knowledge of English, or outside family support. I remember working at a local supermarket when I was nine years old as a way to help my mom make ends meet. I brought home thirty to forty dollars a day, which was a lot of money for someone my age. Some years I attended three different schools because my mother bounced around so much.

My family never had time to go to church; we were preoccupied with surviving. I was never taught about church life or church expectations. We were taught to be spiritual and have respect for God, but that was all. I remember being angry at the sight of kids going into the local church building. They seemed to be part of happy families, and my siblings and I weren't; they had a place to go and we didn't. All we had was trouble and more trouble.

Domestic violence, drugs, gangs, and street violence were lifestyle choices I observed from childhood. In my young innocence and ignorance, I promised my mother that I would never give in to those things—that I wanted nothing to do with that lifestyle. Little did I know how easily I would become a juvenile delinquent.

Since violence was the norm in my community, running with a gang was natural, and being part of a gang had its privileges. Membership meant acceptance, security, power, and respect; especially if you were a leader, as I knew I had the potential for. However, those privileges also had a price tag. For me the price tag was prison. But prison was also where I became a Christian.

I gave my life to Jesus Christ on February 10, 1991, while doing a two-year prison sentence at La Cuchara prison in Ponce, Puerto Rico. I had been on the run from rival gang members in New York City who were trying to kill me. But when I arrived in Puerto Rico I got into stealing cars and stripping them down to sell the parts. The underground market for stolen cars was strong, and the demand was always high. My prison time was for stealing three police cruisers.

While I was in prison, an older lady came and shared the gospel with me. For the first time, I felt like someone was speaking to my heart. Since then, I've dedicated my life to working with the next generation of young people in gangs and in prisons.

Although I attended several first-generation traditional churches, I was never accepted by any of them. Since I wasn't brought up in the church, I had no understanding of church culture. I felt neglected, lost, and abandoned by the church. I was angry at the fact that I prayed, fasted, read the Word, and lived the life more than most of the other kids in the church, but because I didn't fit their image of a Christian, I was never accepted by them. To them I was a sinner and a fake because I was different.

As a result, I started my own ministry. I got together with several friends who had also given up the gang lifestyle to become Christians, and we began to hit the streets, sharing Jesus with people. During this time, God really grew our faith. There were times we would go seven days a week to different churches (most of them either second-generation Hispanic or non-Hispanic churches). We would fast on Sundays and sometimes go to three or four services on that day alone. We were young and fired up for God.

Eventually, though, we went our separate ways, and I ended up in a Spanish-speaking church by the name of Congregación Leon de Juda (Lion of Judah) in Boston. This church was different from the others. It was a large church with a lot of young people who were more like me. The first time I went to their youth group the youth pastor hugged me. At first I felt uncomfortable, but once I got used to it, I felt loved and accepted.

This church willingly took me in as part of their family. Following the Sunday service a few days later, the senior pastor shook my hand and asked my name. I was impressed. But I was even more impressed by the love I was continually shown there with each passing week.

By the time I arrived at Lion of Judah, God had already begun to work on some deep transformations in my life, but the treatment I received from the pastor and church community set that into full speed. I also established meaningful relationships with men and women who mentored me in how to be a man of integrity and Christlike character, and who challenged my personal and spiritual growth as well as held me accountable. It was their loving care that I credit for my pursuing higher education, establishing a healthy marriage and family, and beginning a youth ministry to troubled teenagers.

Key Elements of Urban Hispanic-American Youth Ministry

I believe there are many other unchurched and troubled teenagers with similar backgrounds to my own who would be receptive to the message of salvation if they could just find a truly welcoming church congregation. Lion of Judah was a good "fit" for me because it was largely made up of young Americanized Hispanic families and singles, many of whom were well-educated professionals. The church also was family-oriented and gave me direct access to the pastor; all these elements were very important to me. I'd like to outline three other elements that are important as well.

Understanding, Embracing, and Respecting Cultural Differences

One of the most common mistakes people make in working with Hispanic-American youth is to lump everyone into the same category. The Hispanic-American community is a diverse population comprised of people from many different backgrounds, histories, cultures, and social experiences.

Many people assume that because we have similar names or complexions, we come from the same place or have the same background. Second- and third-generation youth in the United States are usually English-speaking, but many come from homes where Spanish is the only language spoken. As they adapt to the school system and desire to fit in to the dominant culture, many of these children choose English as their first language. It's important to remember, however, that though they may speak English first, many are highly attached to their cultural norms and family values.

Even though there is great diversity within Hispanic culture, there is a growing united Hispanic identity, especially among second- and third-generation Hispanic-American youth. It is this common identity that I want to focus on in this chapter.

The Importance of Relationships

Hispanic-American culture places great value on hospitality, relationships, and family. It's critical for any ministry that is trying to reach Hispanic Americans to be strategic and intentional about the relational aspects of its ministry. Jesus was a master at relational ministry. His whole paradigm of developing his disciples was based around relationships. He ate with them, traveled with them, and spent great amounts of individualized time with each one of them.

Several years ago, I was ministering to a Hispanic young man from the streets, helping him understand manhood and Christlike character. We were sitting in McDonalds when I reached over to him and said, "I am going to talk to you as your pastor." He reached over to me and replied, "I don't need a pastor, I need a father." In that moment I realized that my role with this young man had to be different; he was looking for a family relationship, not a spiritual adviser.

Such Hispanic youth and their families need to feel that their relational needs are being met, that their ministry leaders are accessible. They need to feel that they are an important factor in the life of the church or ministry.

They function best in, and are used to, a relational life. That's how they communicate and that's how they bond.

We are also a very affectionate culture. We are a community of people who enjoy fellowshipping with each other; we refer to one another as family, even those we don't know so well. While we may not be related, we still consider ourselves family and take care of each other as family. Our gatherings can almost seem like reunions; even a first-time visitor to one of these gatherings would feel accepted and like part of the family.

Getting Past the Hype and Hypocrisy

Many in today's society have assumed an image of young Hispanic men and women that oftentimes reflects negatively on our culture. The media promote our machismo and hot temper, but most of all they exploit our sexuality. While these may be legitimate characteristics related to our ethnicity, these issues alone fail to do justice to who we really are as a culture.

The machismo attitude is derived from a traditional lifestyle in which men controlled their wives and their homes. This male chauvinistic behavior has damaged many Hispanic families. Nevertheless, *el machismo* remains important for many adolescent males. This attitude continues to be encouraged and modeled by adult males as well as the media. It manifests itself as young Hispanic males act overly possessive of girlfriends, practically regarding them as their own exclusive property. Conflicts arise when a boyfriend sternly chastises his girlfriend for having any friendships with other boys. In the past girls who resisted such treatment were regarded as rebellious and disrespectful.

While it is no excuse for poor or criminal behavior, many Hispanic youth carry lots of cultural anger and unresolved issues in their lives. Subconsciously they are frustrated at the fact that they just "can't make it." This attitude frequently expresses itself in seemingly random hot-tempered fits of rage.

Compounding this is the fact that many first-generation Hispanic parents feel they cannot effectively control or discipline their children. Though they try, they're at a loss for how to do it. Due to a limited knowledge of English, most Spanish-speaking parents are unaware of the resources that are available to them for support or counseling.

But perhaps the strongest issue in the Hispanic community is that of teen sexuality. Their natural bent toward affection often knows few boundaries when it comes to crossing over into sexual sin. Larry Acosta, executive director of the Hispanic Ministry Center in Santa Ana, California, has labeled teen sexuality as one of the most culturally and spiritually difficult issues for today's church leaders to deal with.[2]

The Role of the Hispanic Church

The vast majority of Hispanic churches today remain far removed from effectively meeting the real needs of second- and third-generation Hispanic families. Most are extremely legalistic, making it nearly impossible for the average street youth to gain acceptance. They are so heavenly minded that they are of no earthly good. Many place rigid emphasis on attendance at Sunday and midweek services, yet lack any outreach programs at all.

At the same time, most Hispanic churches cater only to adults. As a result, many youth fall through the cracks or leave the church altogether because their needs are not being met.

Practical Suggestions for Reaching Hispanic-American Youth

Conduct Contemporary Worship Services

Music has a heavy influence on all teenagers, but this is especially true for Hispanic youth, as music is one of our strongest forms of expression. Latin music is very rhythmic, highly energetic, and conducive for dancing. At the same time it is full of passion and sentimentality. Therefore, Hispanic youth are much more easily brought into a genuine expression of praise and worship when it incorporates these stylistic elements at a contemporary level.

Included in the delivery of praise and worship is the factor of language. Hispanic youth are very proud of their heritage and welcome the incorporation of their native language in worship. Even those who are not proficient will take pride in being able to worship God in Spanish. The most effective Hispanic youth ministries conduct their worship services primarily in English but incorporate Spanish as well. Hispanic youth have trained ears for switching back and forth between both languages. Most are considered proficient in "Spanglish."

Establish Rite-of-Passage Activities

Traditionally, female teenagers are granted a rite-of-passage ceremony, called a *Quinceanero*, at the age of fifteen. This is similar to the Jewish bat mitzvah. The ceremony begins with a church service and is followed by a very elaborate celebration where the *quinceanera* wears a ball gown with a tiara, publicly exchanging her flat shoes for high heels. She is accompanied by fourteen couples of her closest friends, dressed in formal wear and trained to dance a traditional waltz.

During the ceremony the young woman is presented to family and friends as no longer a girl, but a woman. Such ceremonies became popular in the days when teenage girls were expected to take on more adult responsibilities, including marriage.

Most teenage girls are no longer expected to pursue the same time frame for such achievements as their earlier ancestors did, however. In fact, I have seen far too many teenage girls thrown into an adult mentality through such cultural rituals—particularly sexually—when they were not prepared for it.

In response, at Lion of Judah, we have replaced *quinceaneros* with a dedication ceremony in which males as well as females undergo a no-nonsense training adapted from the "True Love Waits" curriculum. They learn about sexual purity according to Scripture. Youth are mentored individually through the process and are challenged to make commitments to remain sexually pure until marriage. Their commitments are celebrated publicly at a formal church service and are followed by a banquet. Young people then choose to wear rings on their fingers as symbols of their commitment.

Develop Small Groups

Because Hispanics are so relational, discipleship happens best in the context of close relationships. The most effective method I have seen is through the use of small groups. However, we do have a cultural stronghold that can work against the success of such groups.

We have a *dicho* (a saying) that says, *"El que diran,"* which is translated, "What others might say." When Hispanic young people do something shameful, the first thing they often hear from their parents is *"El que diran!"* This can send the message that parents are more concerned about perception and honor than about the present condition of their children.

As a result of being taught that what goes on at home stays at home, Hispanic youth may not easily "open up" unless they feel secure and loved. A small-group ministry, however, can go a long way toward allowing Hispanic youth to express themselves and share their issues once they are assured that what they share will be held in strictest confidence.

Minister to the Whole Person

Inner-city Hispanic youth generally lack the social and economic resources necessary to help them prepare for adulthood. In response, some Hispanic churches have incorporated higher education resource centers to assist youth in such areas as preparing for college entrance exams, financial aid, and college retention. Others have established job-training centers for those youth who do not choose a college education. Still other churches have established Bible study groups for post–high school young adults who otherwise typically drop out of church altogether.

Purely social and recreational activities such as field trips, dinners, sleepovers, and hiking also have their place in meeting the needs of Hispanic kids, as do outreach events such as multimedia rallies with dynamic speakers, concert-style worship, and special presentations. In addition, troubled Hispanic youth and those caught up in the juvenile justice system benefit tremendously from youth ministers willing to advocate and walk alongside those truly desiring to better themselves while incarcerated.

Offer Opportunities to Lead

Because Hispanic youth are very relational by culture, creating opportunities for them to invest in others is critical. Through leading, these young people discover and develop their spiritual gifts or begin to discern their own call to ministry. As youth workers allow their youth to become involved in leadership, they quickly discover the inherent strengths in each of their teenagers and have a unique opportunity to encourage them toward deeper maturity.

Working with Hispanic-American youth is certainly one of the most rewarding things I have had the privilege of being involved in. I have consistently seen in them a refreshing genuineness and a realness about their faith. And when they have surrendered their lives to the Lord, they become excited and enthusiastic in worship, passionate in their lifestyle, and committed to seeing others experience God in the same way they have. May God bless you as he grants you the opportunity of laboring in this vineyard as well.

Endnotes

[1] CNN, "Hispanic Population Booms in United States" (March 12, 2001).

[2] Larry Acosta, Mary Arias, and Claudia Ramos, "Hispanic Teens and the Sexual Dilemma," SHOUT Magazine, (Issue Number 2, 1999).

Chapter 7 Ministering to Southeast Asian-American Youth and Families

Ken Gordon

My wife and I felt a calling from God to minister to Cambodians after a two-week mission trip we took together in the late 1980s. We headed from Boston, where we had both grown up, to a Bible college in Minnesota in preparation for a lifetime of missionary service in Cambodia. But instead of sending us to Cambodia after graduation in 1992, God sent us back to Massachusetts, to the city of Lowell.

Known as the "birthplace of the industrial revolution," by the 1840s Lowell had become the second-largest city in New England as well as the industrial center of America. Work was plentiful and, as a result, many immigrant groups relocated to the area. The textile industry began waning in the mid-1900s, and today the mills are shut down; but many immigrant groups such as Southeast Asians still found Lowell to be a welcoming place to make their homes. Today, approximately 25,000 Cambodians live in this city of just over 100,000 people. Lowell has the second-largest Cambodian population of any U.S. city, having been designated by the government as a resettlement area for Cambodians and other Southeast Asian groups in the early 1980s.[1]

As I began to familiarize myself with the city and many Southeast Asian families, I saw the greatest area of need among the teenagers. God was beginning to bring clarity to us regarding the calling he had placed on our lives those many years earlier. He had called us to minister to Southeast Asian teenagers and children, and Lowell was the place we would do that.

Historical Background

One evening, while watching the local news, I saw Sunly, a man I had worked with years earlier when we first moved to Lowell. Sunly's son had just been shot and killed by a local gang, and he was being interviewed by a news reporter.

I went to work to find out where Sunly lived and went to visit him and his family. I met with Sunly and his family many times over the following weeks and months to talk and pray with him. As I did he began to share more openly with me. He said he wished he had never come to the United States. Feeling guilty for having moved his family, he said he should have just stayed in his own country, or what was left of it.

Countless parents like Sunly carry the same feelings. He, like many others, fled Cambodia following the 1975 takeover of Phnom Penh by the Khmer Rouge, when somewhere between one and three million Cambodians died from torture, overwork, or malnourishment—virtually exterminating the educated middle class.

Sunly and his family were able to escape the genocide and reach the Thailand border, where refugee camps were established. It took several weeks to get to the border, and for much of the journey he had to carry his children on his back. Life back then was about survival, and amazingly Sunly had survived. But having escaped the horror of the "killing fields" in Cambodia did not assure his family's safekeeping; the son he had carried on his back fifteen years earlier was now slain on the streets of America. While not all Cambodian families are torn apart by such urban bloodshed, many Cambodian parents like Sunly's grieve over the loss of their children to American culture.

Understanding the Issues

Low-paying jobs, language barriers, the struggle to make ends meet, large families, and coping with the traumas of recent war in Cambodia have left many parents with depleted emotional resources for their children. At the same time, their children and youth are feeling torn between two cultures. As a result, domestic violence and addictions overshadow large numbers of Cambodian homes. Many of the children turn to gangs and become involved in auto theft, drugs, homicide, and other crimes. The most prevalent juvenile delinquent behavior is running away from home, especially among Cambodian girls.[2]

Many Americans mistakenly view Southeast Asians as a single people group, when in fact they have many cultural differences. And while there is no one clear-cut approach that will reach each ministry need in the Southeast Asian community, there are some basic principles that apply to any ministry seeking to reach out to the Asian community.

Culture encompasses values, lifestyle, and social norms—including different communication styles, mannerisms, styles of dress, family structure, traditions, time orientation, response to authority, and more. These differences may be associated with age, religion, ethnicity, and socioeconomic background. A lack of understanding and appreciation for cultural diversity can make people judgmental and limit the opportunity to develop a trusting relationship.[3]

We all have some biases due to our cultural backgrounds. These biases may be positive, negative, or both. Without us realizing it, however, these biases limit our effectiveness in ministering to others. It took me a while to realize that within my culture were traditions or learned behaviors that severely limited my ability to understand the Cambodian culture. I had to learn to be flexible and willing to make sacrifices.

As in many situations, knowledge is the key to understanding. For example, here are a few descriptions of some aspects of traditional Cambodian culture that were foreign to me:

Cambodian Culture

- A man cannot touch a woman in any way to show friendship or affection. Social mixing of the sexes is viewed as improper, and females hide the fact that they may have male friends.

- Cambodians greet by putting their hands together in front of the chest, called "Sampiess." They also greet older people before younger people.

- Marriages are arranged; traditionally, there is no honeymoon. The couple lives with the groom's family. It's not unusual for a Cambodian to marry his or her cousin, niece, or uncle.

- Three or four generations often live together; elders are well cared for by younger family members.

- Parents exercise authority over every area of their children's lives.

- Parents rarely give their children verbal encouragement or thanks.

- Boys and girls ages eleven and twelve are very responsible and are given the care of household, financial, and communication tasks.

- When Cambodians say "yes," they don't necessarily mean that they agree; they may want to be polite or to not lose face.

- Older people's ideas are considered the right ones; ideas young people have are considered immature and are not well accepted.

- Sitting higher than an elder is impolite, as is crossing one's legs, stepping over feet, throwing an object to give it to someone, or placing feet on a table.

- Single people are considered immature, no matter their age.

- Cures for sickness include food sacrifices to spirits, using a suction cup on the skin, and burning the skin. Herbal or root medicines are preferred to western ones.

- Cambodians sit on a reed mat on the floor to eat their meals, rather than at a table.

- Parents do not have contact with schools but instead consider that they are respectfully entrusting their children to the teachers' care.[4]

In addition, I have observed a small altar to deceased relatives in many homes and businesses, containing photographs as well as incense and food offerings.

While the above information specifically applies to Cambodians in Cambodia, there are many cultural differences that apply to other Southeast Asian countries. You will have do some work in researching your specific people group. Keep in mind that you may learn a lot about another culture, lifestyle, or people group, but you will never be from that group.

It is also important to realize that cultural understanding is not something you can learn just from a textbook. You must go into a community and meet people. As you get to know people and form relationships, ask them politely about their background. Where are they from? What is life like at home or school? Ask about their family and friends. Visit them in their homes, eat their food, try to learn their language and culture.

I have found that simply making an effort to learn about Cambodian culture has opened many doors—whether it's having people teach me their language, hearing an individual's personal story of how he or she came to the United States, looking at family photos, or eating traditional Cambodian food. This cultural participation has also opened many opportunities for me to minister to other family members.

I've also made many mistakes. I had always expected eye contact when talking to people, not realizing at first that it is disrespectful for a younger person to look an older person in the eyes when speaking. Also a simple pat on the head is an insult, even to younger children. I have done that many times and have had to apologize later. Once when my wife and I were invited to a friend's house, he met us at the door, grabbed my hand, and showed me around. He brought me into every room, all the while holding my hand. I felt a little awkward, but later learned that this was very customary to his culture.

Religious Differences

A major challenge when ministering to Asians is understanding the influence of their religion. Most Southeast Asians consider Buddhism their religion. Buddhism, however, is not just a religion; it's a way of life. To have any understanding of Southeast Asians, it is critical to understand what makes a Buddhist think the way he or she thinks. This is difficult, though, since Buddhism considers Westerners to be outsiders.

This is the biggest obstacle that any Christian who wishes to minister and present the gospel of Jesus Christ to Southeast Asians must face. And the extent to which the gospel is accepted is largely determined by how an individual chooses to address this difference. Either we can appreciate and accept Buddhism for its values and thought process, or we can condemn Buddhists for being heathens and idolaters. I believe the former is the best approach but would like to distinguish the fact that acceptance does not mean approval.

Donald Posterski, in his book *Reinventing Evangelism*, illustrates this point very well. He uses the example of how the Apostle Paul genuinely accepted and appreciated the Athenians even though he did not agree with them (Acts 17:16-23). Posterski states, "Acceptance is not approval" and "Acceptance does not compromise our spiritual convictions."[5]

Cross-Cultural Adaptation

Many families that have recently immigrated to the United States to begin a new life survive by adapting to American culture while clinging to their own as well. Some survive from day to day while dealing with the effects of post-traumatic stress disorder. Some struggle with survivor's guilt, asking themselves why they were not killed while friends and relatives were. Others develop a variety of other distinct reaction patterns.

Second-generation children (the first generation born in a new country) usually don't like their parents' insistence that they follow the "old ways." They may be ashamed of their original culture and its traditions. They may be ashamed of their parents as well.[6]

Lypor Tea-Chhor, a former participant in the Lowell Mission Youth Church where I have ministered for many years, shared her thoughts in an essay, "Two Cultures, One Life."

"Looking through the eyes of the Cambodian youth today, I can see the struggles and conflicts they and their families go through. Every family has its own issues and problems—Cambodian families experience difficulty living both the American and Cambodian culture....

"Not only is it hard for parents to adapt to the American culture, but most parents do not agree with certain American lifestyles. It breaks their hearts and tradition to see their children living the American way. Most parents are afraid that their children will forget the Cambodian language, tradition, and beliefs. It is difficult for them to accept the fact that their children want to and will live the American way."[7]

Add to this the struggle most adults have with an emotional and traumatic past, and one can understand why it is so hard for them to express their feelings. Many Cambodian children and teenagers do not know what their parents experienced while escaping from the genocide. Some teenagers have told me that their parents wished they had never brought them to the United States. One teen said his parents told him they wished they had left him in Cambodia to die.

These cultural differences often cause tremendous conflicts between parents and their children. Parents may have difficulty learning the American culture, while their youth and children adapt easily. In addition, many parents work long hours and do not spend much time with their children, causing their children to feel neglected or not cared for. Some parents aren't involved with their children's education yet want them to succeed. Many parents are strict about their children's social lives and do not allow dating or any social life at all, while their children desperately desire a social life that includes dating, hanging out with friends, or joining after-school activities.

These conflicts, combined with the inability of parents to express their feelings, cause many youth and children to seek love and acceptance elsewhere. They turn to gangs, drugs, and sex to find love or to try to fit in so others will accept them.

I know many teenagers who are in gangs, and I have observed that most are just looking to be accepted—to be part of a family. We have developed a church for young Asian gang members because there is no other place they feel accepted. They don't hesitate to come to church activities, and once they are away from their usual environment I notice a difference in attitude. They let their guard down a little. If given some respect, they will respect you; however, they must be shown and taught how to ultimately respect God, which is a slow and gradual process.

Many of those who have turned to drugs, sex, or gangs feel they are not "good enough" to become Christians. We must teach them that no one will ever be good enough, but with God's help we can become "new creations." They need someone to encourage, teach, and help them along in their Christian walk. This is often difficult, as each of them needs a positive, one-on-one discipleship relationship. Certainly Christ's words ring out loud and clear: "The harvest is plentiful but the workers are few" (Matthew 9:37).

Relationships Over Programs

Programs, buildings, and people are all mere vessels God can use to minister to others. This was a lesson God taught me four years ago when a fire ravaged our youth church building. As a result, city officials closed it down. God showed me how I had become more dependent on the building than on him for the ministry. I was relying more on our programs to bring people in than on the Holy Spirit's direction. I had to be emptied of my own thoughts, desires, and strength in order to rely upon God's all surpassing strength. Unfortunately, it took the loss of our building and programs to reveal that to me. But as we began to rebuild on more solid footing, the fruit became more abundant too.

Relationships are always the key to effective ministry. First is our relationship with God. We must be in constant communication with him. Next are our relationships with the Body of Christ, showing love to each other. Jesus said, "All men will know that you are my disciples, if you love one another" (John 13:35). Last are our relationships with those we are ministering to. As we live out our Christian lives before them, they begin to grasp what it's all about and how it can work for them.

The Big Picture

If I were to summarize what I have learned over these years of ministry, I would share five pieces of advice. First, know specifically where God wants you to minister. My wife and I have known for a long time that God has called us to minister to Cambodians. We weren't always so sure of the place that would best happen, but we never wavered in the calling. God will place a burden upon your heart for a certain area of ministry. This may happen during prayer or in your quiet times of seeking him. It may also become clear as you step out in different ministry opportunities. But knowing this has been so important to us, as those stressful and difficult times tempt you to just quit otherwise. But every time we get discouraged, as we pray we are quickly reminded that our calling is from God and we need to depend on God and God alone. If there's no specific call, be ready to serve God where you are.

Second, gather as much prayer and support as possible from family and friends (see Colossians 4:3-4; 2 Chronicles 7:14; 2 Thessalonians 1:11-12). This is so important and yet often the most difficult to obtain. I know from personal experience how hard it is to stay focused, and how much I need the prayer and support of others. Apart from that, I'm not sure I would have been able to stay the course.

Third, be flexible and make sacrifices while ministering. Challenges will arise and God will reveal things that he wants you to do or change. These may be difficult to accept if you get too attached to your particular location or methods.

Fourth, gather a united team to minister alongside. Having a common vision and purpose for the ministry is essential. Conflicts will come, but many are diminished if you are all on the same page. Make every effort to encourage one another and hold each other accountable in love.

Last, know the role God wants you to play. Is he directing you to a particular harvest field? Or does he want you to pray for and support others who are sent out to those harvest fields? Wherever or whatever God wants you to do, step out in faith and he will provide!

Endnotes

[1] All information gathered from www.lowell.com Web site.

[2] *Juvenile Offenders and Victims. 1999 Annual Report*, Lowell Police Department Crime/Intelligence Analysis Unit.

[3] One to One/The Mass Mentoring Partnership, *Mentoring 101* (Boston, MA: One to One/The Mass Mentoring Partnership), 15a.

[4] One to One/The Mass Mentoring Partnership, *Mentoring 101*, 20-25.

[5] Donald Posterski, *Reinventing Evangelism* (Markham, Ontario: InterVarsity Press, 1989), 71.

[6] One to One/The Mass Mentoring Partnership, *Mentoring 101*, 15b.

[7] Lypor Tea-Chhor, "Two Cultures, One Life" (essay, Lowell Mission Youth Church, 2000).

Chapter 8
Ministering to Native American Youth and Families

Charles Harper

The frigid winter air and the snowpack on the two-lane highway brought new freshness to this Arizona desert of sagebrush, sandstone monuments, trailer homes, sheep corrals, pickup trucks, satellite dishes, and gang-graffiti-decorated water tanks and windmills. To the outsider, this land would appear useless and void of any opportunity. But this land has been home to thousands of *Dine* (meaning "the people" in Navajo) for as long as anyone can remember.

Here at the foot of one of the Navajo four sacred mountains, missionaries and Native Christian leaders have gathered for refreshing and renewal for at least a hundred years; but this weekend would be the first gathering of Native youth leaders (all part-time volunteers) to strategize ways to reach and disciple Native youth with the gospel.

Michael is emerging as the leader with his humor and ability to keep discussions on track; John attended Bible college for six years and wants to work in full-time ministry among his people but lacks the necessary financial support to do so; Keith is a criminal investigator with the tribal police department; Kevin and Thomas round out the group. We discuss the needs of Native young people on Indian reservations across America, and the meetings are a great success. But I will never forget the challenge issued by one of the elders: "What about the Indian kids in the cities? You know," he said, "the majority of our people now live in the cities."

Though his words were obvious, they still hit us as an entirely new concept. Sure, I know many Indians in cities like Chicago, Los Angeles, Denver, and Minneapolis. And I know several pastors who work with Native people in the cities; I've even done some ministry there myself. But targeting Native American kids in the cities? That was something entirely different.

This chapter takes a brief look at several factors that have brought Native young people to our cities and offers some key principles for reaching them with the gospel.

Historical Background

As European settlers "discovered" the Americas, it's generally accepted that the indigenous peoples were sovereign, strong militarily, and numbered in the millions. But the combination of wars, death, disease, starvation, and forced relocation of Indian tribes to reservations through the mid-1800s nearly wiped out their numbers, spirit, health, and way of life. Many of today's Native Americans refer to those early years of American history as the "American Holocaust."

Just what was in the minds of these early European settlers concerning these native inhabitants of America? Fergus M. Bordewich, in his book *Killing the White Man's Indian*, quotes one Virginia poet after the Jamestown war in 1622, who declared all Indians to be irrevocably "Rooted in Evill, and opposed in Good; errors of nature, of inhumane Birth, The very dregs, garbage and spanne of Earth."[1] Horace Greeley, then editor of the New York Tribune, described their society as belonging to "the very lowest and rudest ages of human existence...These people must die out—there is no help for them."[2] How else could such "good Christian men" justify the slaughter of so much humanity, except to demonize their very nature?

But more recently, the Native American population has been gaining ground: 2000 U.S. Census figures estimate the Native American population at 2,448,000, compared to 1,878,000 in 1990.[3] There are more than 550 federally recognized North American Indian tribes. The largest Indian reservation is the Navajo reservation, which is about the size of West Virginia and extends into three states (Arizona, Utah and New Mexico). Collectively, these tribes amass a total land base of more than 56 million acres.[4]

But according to the National Council of Urban Indian Health, 60 percent of Native American/Alaska Natives live off-reservation in the United States; and of that number more than half (53 percent) live in cities.[5]

Demographics

After the last of the Indian wars had been fought, treaties were signed between the U.S. government and Indian tribes. In exchange for millions of acres of land, the U.S. government would provide for the health, education, and welfare of Indian people.[6]

In the mid-1900s the U.S. government began to recognize the disparity in employment and economic opportunities between those who lived on Indian reservations and those in the dominant society. So in 1934, the Bureau of Indian Affairs initiated the Indian Reorganization Act, which offered employment assistance, one-way bus fares, temporary low-cost housing, and new clothing to anyone willing to leave the reservation and relocate to urban areas. When the Relocation Act was terminated, many Native people had relocated to urban areas. But many others had moved back to reservation life, having never tasted the hoped-for economic advantages.[7]

It's important to note, however, that not all Native people relocate to cities today out of despair and economic hardship. Hundreds of young people have moved there for education and done very well. Many others reside in urban centers as successful businesspeople, professionals, and officials.

Still, Native people are dogged by many alarming statistics. According to the Indian Health Service, the incidence of suicide among Native Americans is 72 percent higher than the rate for all ethnic groups. Among those fifteen to twenty-four years of age, Native American suicides are two and a half times the national rate. The alcoholism death rate among Native Americans is over seven times the U.S. rate for all races. The average life expectancy at birth for Native Americans is 4.7 years less than the life expectancy for all races.[8]

In spite of increased access to education, Native American students feel disconnected from mainstream America and drop out of high school at a rate of 55 percent. Barely 7 percent of Indians graduate from college—less than half the proportion of other Americans.[9]

According to the U.S. Census Bureau, Native Americans are among the most poverty-stricken people in the United States. Between 1998 and 2000, 25.9 percent of American Indians and Alaska Natives were living below the poverty level.[10] While it is true that Indian gaming laws have created opportunities for economic self-determination for some tribes, less than 25 percent of all tribes benefit from casino revenues.[11]

Churches on Indian reservations are struggling and some are even closing. Most lack the essential leadership and membership support needed to flourish and impact those around them. Because the focus of most Native churches is sheer survival, youth ministry and evangelism are virtually ignored.

Issues Facing Today's Native Youth

The social structure in Native America is complex. In the past, extended families served as a safety net for providing for the needs of each member. But today, families are devastated. Single-parent units are the norm. Youth are rapidly turning to gangs, violence, sex, and suicide. Meet one of them— Victor Lopez.

"My name is Victor Lopez. I am a 19-year-old *Dine* ex-gang member. Before I became a Christian, I was living in a world of violence, drugs, gangs, alcoholism, abuse, paint sniffing, and death. My father died from alcoholism when I was eleven years old. It was hard, but I still had my thirteen-year-old brother. Then a year later my brother was shot and killed in a gang incident.

"My brother had two best friends—Benny and Luis. I used to see them around my house with my brother, getting high or drunk. Benny was with my brother when he died. He told me he saw him lying in the alley with a hole in his back, breathing his last breath. That was when Benny became my best friend. Luis came over after my brother's death and told me he missed my brother. He told stories about things they had done together and got sad as he was telling them. We soon became close friends too.

"I had accepted Jesus Christ as my Savior years earlier when I attended a neighborhood kids club at the age of eight. After my brother died, though, I started running the streets. I had a heart for people, but I felt like it left me only showing weakness. I told myself, 'My brother didn't care, so why should I?'

"In our neighborhood there was no shortage of drugs, gangs, prostitution, abuse, pregnant teenagers, mothers strung out on crack cocaine, abused children, and people getting shot—often by their own family members and homeboys.

"At fourteen I became a father, even before I was a man. Then in 1998 Benny was sentenced to three and a half years in prison, and five months later Luis committed suicide. I didn't understand why so many bad things were happening to me. But I can see now that it was a wake-up call from the Lord. In and out of juvenile hall myself, I really wanted to change, especially now that my girlfriend was pregnant. I wanted to be a good father and not abandon my new baby like I had the first baby.

"But I didn't know how to really change. Nine months later my newborn baby died. I was lost and confused and even tried to commit suicide. One night when I was drunk and angry, I stole a car and found myself in the same situation as my best friend who had died. And that's the way I wanted to go out. I figured I'd die that night and wake up in the morning in heaven, shaking my best friend's hand and holding my baby. But I didn't die; the Lord spared me, just as he had so many times before. I went back to paint sniffing, robbing houses, and selling drugs. I was trapped and couldn't save myself.

"One morning, after drinking all night, I looked at myself in the mirror and said, 'There's got to be a better life.' I prayed for God to help me—to change me, to protect me, and to forgive me for all my sins. I didn't think it would work, but something began to happen inside me. I didn't feel like the same crummy person anymore.

"I would like to tell you that my life changed instantly. It didn't, but I have been on a steady track of following the Lord. First, I have been able to forgive my enemies. And I've made amends to those I have so badly hurt. I have asked them to forgive me, and they have. That's given me peace in my heart. I'm becoming involved as a youth leader in the same church I came to Christ in. I see kids that used to be just like me. I don't want them to have to go through the things I went through. I love them like they were my own. It's so incredible for me to receive hugs, respect, and love from them.

"When life is difficult, I go to the Lord. I think about the things I have done and about how God has changed my heart. I have hope and dreams of a future now, for the first time. Like the Scriptures say: ' "For I know the plans I have for you," declares the Lord..."plans to give you hope and a future...You will seek me and find me when you seek me with all your heart" ' (Jeremiah 29:11-13).

"I dream of one day having a family, a car, a home, a wife, and a job. I dream of being a godly man that God will use in other people's lives. My greatest dream is that God would use me to share my testimony so that other young men in jail or on the streets might hear that there is a way out, that there is hope for their lives too, through Christ."[12]

Like Victor, most of today's urban Native teenagers are fashioned by a strong reservation heritage and tradition, yet they face overwhelming stigmas about who they are and where they come from. Sadly, many non-Indian people equate being Native American with alcoholism, trouble, hardship, poverty, and subsisting from government funds and programs—and unfortunately that image greatly impacts how many young Natives begin to see their own destiny.

Urban Native teenagers also struggle with the ability to shift from a Native worldview to a Western worldview and back, depending on the situation. Therefore, a sense of isolation and "not fitting in" becomes overwhelming. When they return to the reservation for a sense of peace and harmony, they realize the degree to which they have been assimilated into Western culture, and often are called "apples" (red on the outside and white on the inside).

Keys to Effective Ministry

When presented with the challenge of writing this chapter, I was overjoyed that such a project was being undertaken, but overwhelmed with feelings of inadequacy, having limited experience ministering in an urban context. In fact, only a small handful have answered the challenge to work with urban Native American kids. I have spent a great deal of time with these unsung heroes, attempting to glean from them some of the nuggets of effective ministry among today's Native American urban teenagers. They are summarized below:

Build Relationships

Among Native people, actions speak much louder than words. Broken treaties and broken relationships down through the generations have contributed to the mistrust that Indian people hold, especially toward non-Indians. Any endeavor that promotes acceptance and trust will be successful. It's easy to establish "programs" and justify the need for housing, education, assistance, social welfare, and other Native entitlements, but more rewarding is the process of gaining mutual trust, acceptance, and respect.

Yet, even among themselves, Native Americans carry a background steeped in broken relationships and damaged trust. It takes intentional effort to build trustworthy relationships, as well as patience, commitment, and integrity. This begins with being a person of your word. Most Native young people have built protective walls and wear invisible masks to hide their pain. It takes time and patience to get to know who they really are. But as they begin to perceive your willingness to go the distance with them and feel respected for who they really are, the fields will be ripe and ready to harvest.

Commitment is an essential element in building relationships for effective ministry. Part of this commitment is just *being there*. A question commonly asked of newer youth workers is "How long will you be here?" Young people are looking for stability. They will begin to let their guard down if they can trust that you will be around for a while.

Commitment also involves a willingness to sometimes be a punching bag for others' frustrations. There is an old proverb that says, "Hurt people hurt people." This is a critical component of the healing process for damaged young people.

Relationships can take place on various levels. One youth leader I know targets kids through their moms. She says it helps both the kid and the parent to respect you more. This is especially true among Native Americans who traditionally maintain an incredible sense of family loyalty. Relationships can also extend to a young person's friends, neighbors, or siblings. Other proven points of entry are through sports and art, or anything else kids may be interested in.

Stress Identity in Christ

Harvey slumps back in the seat of his newly acquired '69 Chevelle with a new candy-apple paint job. "See you later in the barrio, man. I got to go pick up my cousin at the powwow first." He hangs up his cellphone and cranks up the rap music.

Harvey, an urban Native American young person, is living in a world of multi-everything! Externally he has learned to adapt to many pressures, but internally he is seeking for answers.

Society and stereotypical thinking have taught Native kids that it's bad and hopeless to be Indian. Urban Indian youth need to know their greatest identity can be found in Christ. When they understand this, they, like Victor, the ex-*Dine* gang member, can find the peace, purpose, and joy they so long for.

One of the most significant messages I have ever heard on identity came from a Native pastor as he was explaining the three options God gave Joshua and those "tribal people" who were being led from their "reservation" to a new and promised land. God challenged them in Joshua 24:15, "Choose for yourselves this day whom you will serve."

Their first option was to follow the gods of their ancestors, including all of their religious traditions. Their second choice was to choose the gods of the land they were moving into. Today this could be equated with such things as drugs and alcohol, money, technology, and power. A third option was to choose the Lord. And when people choose to serve him, they must serve him and serve him alone. Today's young Native Americans are faced with the same choices.

Without question, the most hotly debated topic in the Christian Church in Native America today is over cultural expression and the use of traditional Native American ceremonial items like eagle feathers, drums, and gourds. While it is important for young people to know their culture and heritage, the most important thing for them to know is who they are in Christ, their creator, and to make him their Lord and source of identity.

One's identity, especially in a Native American context, cannot be separated from worship. In fact, worship is at the core of Native society, culture, and religion. When the true God becomes the recipient of worship, one's true identity comes more sharply into focus with him in whose image we were created (Genesis 1:27). This is an especially important factor when dealing with urban Native youth, for many have lost this sense of worship as they've left their tribal culture and become enmeshed in the city. Yet wherever we have seen young warriors come to Christ and grow deeply in him, Christ-centered worship has been a key element.

Expand Their Vision

God gives each of us special gifts and abilities that benefit the Kingdom of Christ. Great works can be accomplished when such blessings are utilized. Having said that, I believe two factors have hindered the Native church thus far from becoming all that it can be.

First, although Christ's discipleship model of winning, building, and sending has been effective with many cultures and peoples, the church in Native America has not, at least in recent years, been challenged to be a sending people. One Native young person told me that part of the problem stems from the fact that Native people have always been on the receiving end of missions. When paternalistic thinking changes and Native people themselves become the sending agents or "missionaries," their role in Christ's Kingdom will be more fully realized.

Second, the church that many Native young people are acquainted with uses legalistic and guilt-motivated methodologies. One leader told of hearing Native people tell him that many would turn to Jesus if they saw one example of a vibrant Native Christian. However, when young people are encouraged to creatively use their gifts, much can and will happen. Native young people are very creative and resourceful when given the opportunity and can take on a great deal of responsibility when entrusted with it. One Christian leader I know tells of encouraging his teenage daughter to go ahead and start an outreach group. The first person she led to the Lord was a sixty-year-old woman. Another started a Native performing arts group, and a third has led mission trips while still attending high school.

Seek Them Out

Native Americans are often hidden in cities. Most of them live within areas with an ethnic concentration. Some cities, such as Denver, Minneapolis, Omaha, and Chicago, have Indian centers—physical buildings staffed by Natives and offering networking and supportive help.

Once you find them, focus on the primary task that is given to every Christian. God wants all people to come to know and worship him. He calls us to share his life-changing gospel message. Avoid becoming sidetracked with political and social movements. Your role as a Christian youth leader is not to change the environment or culture of Native people, but to see people set free from sin.

The Harvest Is Plentiful

There is a great need today for youth workers among Native American young people, both in urban settings and on reservations. The vast majority of ministries to Native people are focused on adults, while precious little ministry is being carried on with Native youth—even though their age segment comprises the largest percentage of the population. As one Native leader in Phoenix says, "I have access to over a thousand Native students, yet there really is no outreach taking place. It will take more help."

Take the time to see through the eyes of Native Americans. Acknowledge differences in worldviews. Acknowledge that much destruction and many atrocities have taken place in the name of the "white man's God" in the history of American Indian missions and the founding of America. Consider the fact that youth ministry might be best accomplished with Native youth leaders at the helm, and then support a Native youth leader. There are several trained and gifted Native youth leaders who would gladly be in full-time youth ministry but lack financial support.

The reality of Matthew 9:37 couldn't be more true for Native youth ministry today. The harvest indeed is plentiful, yet the workers are few. Pray with me that God would send more workers into the harvest, and ask him what part he might have you play.

Acknowledgments
Special thanks to those who gave valuable time, wisdom, and insight in answering questions and helping in this project:

   Brian Brightcloud, pastor, Los Angeles, California
   Laura Butler, youth leader, Albuquerque, New Mexico
   Casey Church, pastor, Michigan and New Mexico
   Huron Claus, Native ministry, Phoenix, Arizona
   Kit Danley, youth leader, Phoenix, Arizona
   Raymond Dunton (Hopi), pastor/teacher, Ignacio, Colorado
   Dave Gowan, Bible Society, Portland, Oregon
   Mike Hendricks, youth worker, Albuquerque, New Mexico
   Carmell Hill, youth leader, Vancouver, British Columbia
   Jon Lansa (Hopi), youth worker and ministry specialist, Albuquerque, New Mexico
   Larry Littlebird (Laguna, Santo Domingo), Native minister, Albuquerque, New Mexico
   Leon Matthews (Lakota Sioux), pastor, South Dakota
   Leta Rector (Cherokee), writer, Tulsa, Oklahoma
   Roger Scarbro, youth pastor, Gallup, New Mexico
   Craig Smith (Chipewa), church administrator/evangelist, Scottsdale, Arizona
   Deswood Tome (Navajo), Promise Keepers Strategic Alliance Director, Denver, Colorado
   Richard Twiss (Lakota Sioux), ministry specialist, Vancouver, Washington
   Rusty Van Duesen, youth leader, Anacortes, Washington
   Doug Yates (Heida/Shimshan), youth pastor and evangelist, Anchorage, Alaska
   Members at the Chicago Indian Center, Chicago, Illinois
   Students on the streets of Seattle, Washington

Endnotes
   [1] Fergus M. Bordewich, *Killing the White Man's Indian* (New York, NY: Anchor Books, 1997), 35.
   [2] Bordewich, *Killing the White Man's Indian*, 49.
   [3] U.S. Census Bureau Web site, January 2001, http://www.census.gov/population/estimates/nation/intfile3-1.txt.
   [4] U.S. Department of the Interior, Bureau of Indian Affairs Web site, http://www.doi.gov/bia/oirm/faq.htm.
   [5] National Council of Urban Indian Health Web site, http://www.ihs.gov/NonMedicalPrograms/Urban/ncuih/home.html.
   [6] Francis Paul Prucha, editor, *Documents of United States Indian Policy, Second Edition, Expanded* (Lincoln, NE: University of Nebraska Press, 1990), 221-222.
   [7] Prucha, *Documents of United States Indian Policy*, 237-238.

[8] Indian Health Service, "General Mortality Statistics,"
http://www.ihs.gov/PublicInfo/Publications/trends98/part4.pdf.

[9] Bordewich, *Killing the White Man's Indian*, 13.

[10] U.S. Census Bureau, "Number of Poor and Poverty Rate by Race and Hispanic Origin: 1998 to 2000," http://www.census.gov/hhes/poverty/poverty00/tableb.pdf.

[11] U.S. Department of the Interior, Bureau of Indian Affairs Web site:
http://www.doi.gov/bia/oirm/faq.htm.

[12] Personal interview with Victor Lopez, 2001.

Chapter 9
Ministry to Today's Urban Girls
Patricia Coleman Hill and Judy D. Landis

What picture comes to mind when you think about today's urban girl?

Is it someone with a big mouth? a defiant attitude? a readiness to fight at the blink of an eye? hair colors and extensions? tattoos?

How about someone with a joyful outlook on life? a determined spirit to achieve despite incredible odds? a willingness to step into the middle of a disagreement and plead for peace? a love for the Lord and enthusiasm to serve him? a college degree?

There are so many success stories about urban girls alongside the many other tragic ones. In this chapter we will focus on some of the unique challenges of growing up female in urban America and how we can best reach and equip these treasures of God.

Understanding the Issues

Today's urban girls come in all shapes, sizes, personalities, and dispositions. They come from different cultures and struggle with many unique issues. Many quietly, and with great dignity, are defying society's generalized assumptions and stereotypes regarding their womanhood. Unfortunately, they all face the "double jeopardy" of both growing up female in a male-dominated society and often belonging to a minority subculture or socioeconomic group.[1] A great task and critical responsibility await those with a heart for working with young urban women. Following are some of the common issues that many of them share.

Unresolved Pain

Perhaps the most common issue young urban women share with one another is a deep hurt caused by unresolved pain in their lives. The stories are numerous: a stepfather who disciplines by punching or kicking. A mother, consumed by the pressures of daily living, who resorts to hurling verbal abuse. Another mother who sleeps with various men, and despite her daughter's best efforts at keeping the bedroom door locked and a knife under the pillow, she ends up being raped anyway by one of the male visitors.

The "hard" attitude many young women are capable of projecting is a defensive wall, a barricade to protect themselves from being hurt by further pain. The "I'm bad" attitude or acting out is, in reality, a cry from a hurting soul that can't help but shout everything from "Leave me alone" to "Because I hurt, I want everyone and everything else to hurt."

Bianca (not her real name) was a junior high girl who never allowed anyone to "mess with her." She projected a tough image that kept people at a distance. Once, on a youth group trip to the state capitol, Bianca pulled out an eighteen-inch pair of scissors.

"Uh, Bianca, why are you carrying those scissors?" asked the youth leader.

"In case anybody messes with me, I'm going to get 'em."

"Bianca, if anyone messes with you here today, I've got your back. Can I hold the scissors for you?"

She handed over the mini-machete, which stayed in the van for the rest of the day. Though all were able to laugh together about it later, it's sad to consider the level of pain in Bianca's life that would cause her to feel the need to defend herself on a youth group trip—from real or imagined danger—in such a way.

The Struggle for Healthy Cultural Identity

Any member of a cultural minority group, or anyone from the dominant culture who does not live up to societal standards, also shoulders a tremendous ambivalence of identity caused by racism or prejudice. This struggle is tragically misunderstood and minimized by those who benefit from socially acceptable physical characteristics such as skin color, hair style, clothing, and body shape. This issue goes far beyond low self-esteem. Societal institutions, the media, and interpersonal experiences reinforce popular notions that certain hair is too kinky, weight measurements too excessive, skin color too dark, and intellect too dull. Confronting generalized stereotypes that "your kind" is lazy and criminally inclined becomes part of daily living. Thus, the question of "Who am I?" is intensified by the burden of overcoming prejudice and racism.

There are several responses to the struggle for cultural identity. Some young women assimilate into the dominant culture, usually denying the beauty and diverse contributions of their own ethnic heritage. Others completely reject the dominant culture and isolate themselves from it, whether through music, hair and clothing styles, or other cultural expressions. Some choose biculturalism, where they learn to function both in their own culture and in the dominant culture, though often only on a superficial level. Finally, there is the ethnic response, which is a proud acceptance and projection of one's own culture, usually to the exclusion of the diversity of other cultures. In any given group of young women, all four responses may be seen in operation.[2]

Closely related to the struggle for a healthy cultural identity are the second-generation issues of many immigrant groups. Parents who have emigrated from a homeland often retain the use of the language and other cultural traditions in their home life, which younger generations may reject in favor of embracing "American" culture. Inevitably, conflicts arise, both internally within the young person as well as generationally with the parents.

Some young ladies also struggle with their culture's traditional views of women. Women are often pressured not to seek higher education or to seek only certain types of employment. Indeed, for some cultures, only certain types of employment may be available. Many work long hours for low pay, only to have their paychecks turned over to the family so that their brothers can go to school. Many others are not permitted to seek leadership roles within their communities, and some are expected to assume all the duties of household labor and complete care of any children.[3]

Issues of Sexuality

The search for identity is sometimes most visible in how a young woman expresses her sexuality. Many do not see themselves as valuable human beings worthy of protection and respect. Most are looking for someone to love them, even if that love is distorted. What else would cause four girls in one school to sleep with one guy, resulting in three abortions and one baby? "I love him." "He buys me things." "No one else loves me, so I will cling to him and trap him with a baby. If he leaves, I still have the baby," they reason. It's a classic and tragic case of looking for love in all the wrong places and being willing to settle for a few table scraps even though God's design calls for a banquet feast.

An adolescent's understanding of sexuality is often limited to the act of sexual intercourse. In addition, myths like "I can't get pregnant the first time" abound. Many young people also face cultural taboos against speaking openly and honestly about sexual issues. Shame and punishment are associated with sexuality, rather than the values of covenant and commitment.[4] The totality of one's being in sexual intercourse—body, mind, spirit—is rarely taught or emphasized.[5]

The pursuit of "love" and sexual gratification inevitably leads to children. Young mothers struggle with the tremendous responsibility and demands of a baby or babies, requiring much support from family, friends, and social service systems. Child-rearing instruction is generally limited to the young woman's own upbringing, and childcare is often scarce or expensive. In addition, the time and energy invested in raising her child, whom she accepts and loves, can become a hurdle to a young woman's development in other areas such as education, career, and even simply enjoying her own growth into young adulthood.

It is always best for women to be the primary vehicles of ministry to young girls, especially when one considers all the issues of sexuality that are present.

Growing Up in Poverty

Another common struggle for urban girls living in distressed neighborhoods is dealing with poverty's wide-ranging effects. Poverty must be defined as what it really is—a lack of resources.[6] In addition to a lack of financial resources, many families are denied access to decent educational materials, adequate medical care, and employment that both pays a living wage and includes benefits.

According to the National Center for Children in Poverty, over 12 million children in America, the wealthiest nation on earth, are growing up in poverty. Poor children are more vulnerable to everything from inadequate prenatal care and substandard housing, to repeating a school grade due to chronic sickness, family breakdown, and hunger. Seventeen percent of American children live in families with incomes below the federal poverty line.[7] Of course, a great percentage of these children are born to urban teenage mothers. Many such mothers don't have access to a local bank with no minimum requirements on checking or savings accounts. Hence, check-cashing stores gladly charge 15 percent as payment for cashing a minimum-wage paycheck, leaving little for savings. Welfare-to-work programs guarantee work for only six months, and daycare expenses can easily overwhelm even the strictest budget.

Life in poverty-stricken urban areas becomes a daily struggle for survival and a fight to obtain life's most basic needs of food, shelter, and relative safety. Planning for the future is but a dream as a general sense of hopelessness and despair chokes out any ambition to reach for more. The absence of safety nets and precious little overall security can easily compound any normal adolescent identity crisis.

Violence

Violence and gang involvement also plague the lives of many urban girls. According to statistics provided by the Philadelphia Industrial Correction Center, more females than males between the ages of nine and eighteen are now being arrested for violent crimes.[8]

Fighting and mouthing off at each other are the primary means of conflict resolution for many urban girls. Suppressed pain and self-hatred are the fuel that spark many interpersonal conflicts. Reputation is at stake and, rather than working toward peace or harmony, showing that "I'm not a punk" is the normal response. In fact, "watching each other's back" and viewing one another as sisters is overshadowed by hatred and a false view of "she thinks she's better than everyone else."

For many, gang involvement provides the security, support, or even survival needed in the midst of violent environments. Young women join gangs because of peer pressure ("my girlfriend is in it"), a need for control over their own lives or others, the opportunity to be the leader of a group of people, or simply because their parents don't care and they desire a sense of family togetherness. Whatever the reason, joining a gang is usually much easier than leaving one. Better alternatives and options must be provided for these young women.

Religious Confusion

The prevalence of many different religions in urban settings also influences the development of young women. By her teenage years, an African-American young lady may have attended a Pentecostal church with her grandmother, been exposed to the Koran by her Muslim uncle (Islam practiced according to principles in the Koran calls on men to respect and protect women), and watched her aunt faithfully knock on doors in the neighborhood as a Jehovah's Witness. Many Asian women are raised in households adhering to the values and ideals of Buddhism, Taoism, or Confucianism, while Latino girls are exposed to syncretistic variations of the Catholic faith, including Santeria (a mixing of indigenous practices with Catholicism). Confusion over what to believe and who to follow abounds. Given the abundance of challenges facing urban girls, it is a testimony to God's grace that so many develop into strong, lovely, and mature women of God!

Essential Elements for Effective Ministry

The unique pressures placed upon today's urban girls can paint a bleak picture. Yet God has called us to make a difference in the lives of his precious daughters. It is critical that we be adequately prepared for God to use us.

Expand Your Understanding of Cultural Issues

Any person working with urban girls—but particularly those who come from a suburban or rural background—must be willing to allow their own worldviews to be expanded and to abandon any notion that the way they understand the world is the only right way. The most effective way to minister to another is to follow Christ's incarnational example of walking in that person's shoes. Be willing to learn about and understand the world from the urban girl's point of view.

Those who minister to urban girls must become students of the culture within which they are working or, if from the same background, the generation with whom they are working. Each group faces unique challenges and issues that can easily be discovered by reading relevant magazines and books and by simply asking questions and listening! For instance, diverse Asian and Latino cultures emphasize the importance of a strong, communal family life, often influencing the decisions young people make regarding employment and marriage.[9] Understanding the powerful effect of music in reaching African-American youth will be helpful in ministering to African-American young women.[10]

Culture is of primary significance to those who have grown up in a predominately non-Caucasian, urban setting. Daily struggles with racism are very real and extremely painful, and cause much ambivalence regarding identity. Such challenges must be acknowledged, cultural diversity celebrated, and healthy ethnic identities encouraged. Be willing to listen to the stories of those who face the humiliations of racism or prejudice, and resist the temptation to blow off sensitivity to race with a "just get over it" attitude. There are many young women who simply do not have that option!

Nurture Your Own Soul

The need for you to nurture your own personal relationship with Jesus Christ may seem like an unnecessary stating of the obvious. Yet it is amazing how many youth workers rush to the latest ministry gimmick while neglecting their relationships with the Lord. In the midst of overwhelming concerns about today's urban environment, the first thing to do is spend time developing intimacy with God. What works is relationship—with urban girls and ultimately with Jesus Christ. Be willing to ask questions of yourself, such as "Where am I in my relationship with Christ?" "What kind of 'fragrance of the knowledge of' Christ (2 Corinthians 2:14) am I giving off?" "Do others take note that I have been with Jesus (Acts 4:13)?"

Doing is always easier than being. But "doing" on a continual basis can lead to burnout, especially if all our doing produces little visible result. Unless we take the time to allow God to fill us up with himself and his Word, we don't have anything to give, and "doing" soon becomes simply an end in itself. Soon we are relying solely on our own skills and abilities when the Bible teaches us that it is "only God, who makes things grow" (1 Corinthians 3:7b). The power of God works in us and through us only as we tap into our power source.

It is a great temptation to be consumed by the urgency of the needs we see in our urban centers. Yes, the task is endless. Yes, we always need more help. Yes, we can easily work 24/7. However, it is to the detriment of ourselves and those we are called to, when we refuse our Lord's invitation in Matthew 11:29: "Take my yoke upon you and learn from me...and you will find rest."

Program to Reach Them

Churches must be convinced of the importance of young girls and the need to develop specialized ministries to reach them. Opportunities must be given for them to participate meaningfully in the life of the church, or their inevitable exodus will surely result.

Honest, straight talk is vital, not only to understanding where young women are coming from, but in providing an environment where they feel free and secure to share about any aspect of life. Be careful of relaying a "goody two-shoes" attitude, and check for a judgmental spirit, which can cause young women to clam up about some of the things in which they are involved. Be aware that "phonies" are quickly exposed, as urban life is often a raw, "in your face" existence. Being yourself in an atmosphere of unconditional love and acceptance works best. The hardest attitude can quickly be won over through genuine interest, a willingness to listen, and consistency. As young women share their pain, be willing to appropriately hug and hold those who may, for the first time, receive love expressed in a Christlike way.

For Christians who come in contact with girls in a secular environment where Christianity cannot be pushed, be upfront about your spirituality. What makes the MODEL (Made of Divine Excellence and Love) Mentoring Program in Philadelphia so successful in the public school environment is that the staff and mentors all have personal relationships with Jesus Christ. The girls who participate in the program are aware of this fact from the first meeting and are given the option of leaving if they wish—a choice no one has yet decided to make!

Programming elements necessary for effective ministry to urban girls are discussed below:

Spirituality

Spirituality is included as a "rite of passage," along with physical, emotional, and psychological milestones. MODEL Mentoring Program Director Pat Coleman invites her senior pastor to share with the girls about their purpose and destiny. Each one has been given an assignment in this life by the one who created her, and her mentor is committed to helping make that a reality. Hence, the girls respect the mentors and guest speakers in response to the respect they receive. Many end up attending church or pursuing other Bible study activities outside the public school system.

Life Skills Training

Teach young women everything you know, and be willing to research and learn together what you don't. Teach or provide instruction for everything from sexual purity, etiquette, cooking, nutrition, and body and hair care to budgeting and financial investment, gardening, and the roles of wife and mother. Teach biblical principles of celibacy, body maintenance, and money management, even in a secular environment where you cannot specifically say that what you are communicating is biblical wisdom.

You may come across a young woman who was never instructed in the basics of hygiene, something to which other girls will be quick to point. A little one-on-one counseling or a guest who can graciously encourage young women in body and hair care will be helpful. Tap into girls' love of hair colors and styles, nail polish, and body fragrances to teach a lesson from 1 Corinthians 6:18-20 about honoring God with our bodies...including the fact that we are looking good for God, not for the boy down the street!

Do not assume that girls who grow up in economically distressed neighborhoods will know much about budgeting or bank accounts, or cooking or nutrition, for that matter. Many urban neighborhoods are overrun with fast food restaurants, fried chicken establishments, and corner stores selling soda pop and potato chips, all of which make up the bulk of many diets. Cooking is also a fun way to build relationships. Many a great conversation has taken place over a homemade batch of chocolate chip cookies.

Counseling

The provision of biblical counseling services must become a vital part of any ministry to urban youth. In environments where violence is prevalent and post-traumatic stress disorder a reality, such ministry is sadly lacking. When young women grow up attending far more funerals than weddings, they need to talk with someone. Counseling must be taken out of the realm of "those who can afford it" and be made available to all those who so desperately need to make sense of what they experience in daily life.

Youth workers must also understand the legal issues surrounding abuse. You are bound by law to report abuse or suicidal threats, and young women need to know that before they begin sharing with you. Assure them that you care and are willing to do whatever it takes to make sure they will be safe.

Lastly, no ministry addressing the needs of urban girls can flourish without addressing the unique challenges and issues facing urban young men. It does no good to teach abstinence to young women while the young men are roaming around with their pants unzipped. Do whatever possible to provide ministry or services to both genders. After observing the MODEL Mentoring Program, the young men began asking, "When can we have a program, too?"

Christlike Role Models

The most essential element for effective ministry to urban girls involves Christlike role models. Ruth had her mother-in-law, Naomi (see Ruth 1:16-17). Eunice had her mother, Lois (see 2 Timothy 1:5). Paul instructed Titus in Titus 2:3-5 to "teach the older women...Then they can train the younger women."

Too often, youth ministers and youth workers take on themselves all the responsibility of providing the role models young women need. Meanwhile, churches and neighborhoods are filled with both men and women steeped in the wisdom of age who, given the proper training, appropriate boundaries, and reasonable time commitments, would delight in an opportunity to provide spiritual guidance and instruction to the younger generation. This gold mine lies dormant as youth workers struggle with the frustration of too many young people in need of attention and too little time or energy. The time has come for us who work with young people to see ourselves as a means of connection, the builders of relationships among others, rather than as the sole source of relationship.

Cultural considerations are of extreme importance in building one-on-one relationships. To match a young woman with an older woman from the same cultural background who has had similar life experiences provides for a much deeper connection. It is true that someone can have a positive influence on one who is outside her own culture, just as it is also true that within the same culture a one-on-one relationship can be a disaster. God can and does work powerfully through whomever he chooses; however, it is time to humbly acknowledge that perhaps the most effective minister is one who has walked in that person's shoes.

Take the time necessary to recruit and involve others and provide training, especially on the level of certification, so that each girl can receive the individual attention she so desperately needs. The mentors in the MODEL program undergo six weeks of training provided by a citywide mentoring network. They then spend two hours per week with their "mentees" in a group setting and one-on-one interactions during a school-year-long program. Follow-up contact is maintained until the girls' high school graduation. Whether it is called "discipleship" in a church setting or "mentoring" in a secular setting, young women need the positive input and influence of someone older and wiser.

Be sure to include men in the process as well, while being wise about essential boundary issues. A man functioning in his God-given responsibilities serves as both a protector for and a role model of how a young woman should expect to be treated. It is much easier for a girl to respect her virginity if her father or a father figure deems it of infinite value. Though it is difficult in today's climate of perverted relationships to encourage one-on-one interaction between a male role model and a young woman, group interactions should be encouraged, as should married couples serving as role models together.

In their book *The Black Church in the African American Experience*, C. Eric Lincoln and Lawrence H. Mamiya describe the provision of role models as "one of the most important functions that black churches performed for young people."[11] Whether it happens in the context of a mentoring program, rites of passage, cultural instruction, musical ensembles, after-school tutoring, or any variety of programs that can be created, connecting urban girls with God-fearing role models, both male and female, who have a heart and a mind for young people, is absolutely essential.

Partner With Parents

No matter how dysfunctional or absent parents may be, unless they are deceased, every girl still has a father and a mother who need to be respected and honored as such. Encourage young women to pray for their parents and to be loving witnesses to them. Involve parents as much as possible in any relationships with a young woman, never leaving them completely out of the process.

There are instances when a child may need to be removed from her family setting immediately for her own personal safety. However, there are youth workers who, seeing dysfunctional family settings where the environments are not good but the girls are in no immediate danger, want to "rescue" the girls and bring them into their own homes. Proceed with caution and much prayer when attempting to do this, and be sure to consider extended family in the process. There are too many situations where youth workers allow young women to move into their homes, only to have the situations not work out in the end.

Removing a young woman is often the easiest way to "save" her from a troublesome environment. It takes much more time, energy, and commitment—plus a willingness to work toward connecting the family with a church family—to work with a dysfunctional family as a unit in encouraging a more wholesome home atmosphere. In the end, however, keeping the family together provides a much more credible solution.

Program for Fun

Whatever form ministry takes, it is important for young women to have the opportunity for good, clean fun. Many are robbed of the opportunity to fully enjoy childhood and long to relive the pure fun and excitement of running around like children. So, in addition to providing counseling and instruction, make room for some major fun. This doesn't mean just taking an annual trip to the local amusement park. A coloring book and crayons, a sleepover, or the provision of a babysitter for a young woman with children so that she can attend an outing are all wonderful means of having fun. Memorable youth club experiences have included everything from building sand castles on the beach to creating a miniature golf course by using trees as "holes," tennis balls, and a bag of old golf clubs.

Entrust Them to God

The foundation of all ministry is prayer. Our job is not to make the necessary changes in the lives of young women, but to intercede and advocate on their behalf before the Father for wisdom, healing, deliverance, "hope and a future" (Jeremiah 29:11). Ministry to today's urban girls also requires great sacrifice, commitment, and an investment of time and energy. The building of relationships requires our willingness to pour our lives into others, so that they may know that they are "fearfully and wonderfully made" (Psalm 139:14).

Though we usually begin with a desire to teach, give, and minister, inevitably we are the ones who learn and receive the most. We have been blessed to witness young women shedding Muslim garb for a personal relationship with Christ; graduating from college; becoming wives, mothers, and leaders in their communities and churches. Our own lives have been changed by their probing questions, permission to enter their world, and their laughter and love. Their strength under tremendous pressure, dignity in the face of prejudice, deep understanding of God's love, and rich enjoyment of life have opened our eyes and made our hearts more sensitive as we share and learn together with today's urban girls.

Endnotes

[1] The idea of "double jeopardy" for women comes from an essay by Liane Rozzell entitled "Double Jeopardy" in *America's Original Sin: A Study Guide on White Racism*, published and distributed by Sojourners, Box 29272, Washington, DC 20017, 25-27.

[2] Grace Sangok Kim, "Asian North American Youth: A Ministry of Self-Identity and Pastoral Care," in David Ng, Editor, *People on the Way: Asian North Americans Discovering Christ, Culture, and Community* (Valley Forge, PA: Judson Press, 1996), 211-212.

[3] Carmen Maria Cervantes, General Editor, *Prophets of Hope, Volume 1: Hispanic Young People and the Church's Pastoral Response* (Winona, MN: St. Mary's Press, 1994), 42.

[4] Cervantes, *Hispanic Young People and the Church's Pastoral Response*, 60.

[5] An excellent resource which challenges young people, particularly in the African-American community, to consider the totality of their beings in sexual intercourse is the book *Wild Thing: Let's Talk About Sex*, by Haman Cross, Jr., Donna E. Scott, and Eugene Seals (Union City, GA: ICR Publications, 1992).

[6] See John Perkins' discussion of the principle of redistribution in Chapters 15-18 of his book *With Justice For All* (Ventura, CA: Regal Books, 1982), for a fuller understanding of all the dimensions of poverty.

[7] National Center for Children in Poverty Web site, *Child Poverty Fact Sheet (June 2001)*, http://cpmcnet.columbia.edu/dept/nccp/ycpf-01.html.

[8] Philadelphia Industrial Correction Center, Philadelphia, Pennsylvania. Statistics given to the MODEL Mentoring Program on a field trip to the facility in 2000.

[9] See both Cervantes, *Hispanic Young People and the Church's Pastoral Response*, pp. 48-49; and Joan May Cordova, "Historical and Cultural Context," in Donald Ng, Editor, *Asian Pacific American Youth Ministry* (Valley Forge, PA: Judson Press, 1988), 32-33.

[10] C. Eric Lincoln and Lawrence H. Mamiya, *The Black Church in the African American Experience* (Durham, NC: Duke University Press, 1990), 345.

[11] Lincoln and Mamiya, *The Black Church in the African American Experience*, 312.

Chapter 10
Ministering to Today's Juvenile Offender

Dr. Scott Larson

I was recently leading a Bible discussion group in a detention center that I'd been visiting since 1987. I was acquainted with nearly all of the twelve boys who sat there, as most had been in and out of jail several times. Recognizing that a good number of them were gang involved, I asked, "How many of you are in a gang?" Everyone's hand went up. "Why did you join a gang?" I then asked.

I expected to hear responses like "I joined a gang because I thought they'd always be there for me, but now I don't hear from anyone. No phone calls, no letters. Nothing. And one of my boys is hitting on my girl."

Instead, Jason started off with, "I was a nobody when I joined my gang. Now I have respect wherever I go." Tyrone added, "I used to be afraid to go out of the house at night in my neighborhood. Now nobody messes with me." Tommy chimed in, "For the first time in my life I have a goal—something I can strive for. I want to climb up to a position in my gang where everyone knows and respects me. And I'll do whatever it takes to get that."

But perhaps Edwin captured it best when he said, "I was looking for something big enough to live for and big enough to die for. That's what my gang gave me."

By the time they were finished I was ready to join a gang! They had hit on all the things I was looking for too. Then I realized I had a problem. The only thing we were in agreement about was that gangs were the way to go! And that was obviously not my chosen topic for the evening. How could I transition this into something more spiritual and redemptive?

In response to a quick prayer spoken under my breath, I said, "Let me read to you something about the first gang I have ever heard about." They were all ears as I read from Acts 2:43-47:

"Everyone was filled with awe, and many wonders and miraculous signs were done by the apostles. All the believers were together and had everything in common. Selling their possessions and goods, they gave to anyone as he had need. Every day they continued to meet together in the temple courts. They broke bread in their homes and ate together with glad and sincere hearts, praising God and enjoying the favor of all the people. And the Lord added to their number daily those who were being saved."

When I finished, everyone was quiet. Jason was the first to respond. "Yo, that's real." After a few more moments of silence he continued, "That's the church, huh?"

"Yeah," I said.

Another asked, "Do they have a church like that where I live?"

"I don't know," I confessed.

As I left that night, two things stuck out in my mind. First, each of these gang members understood well the description of the early church as it is explained in Acts 2, and they were willing to leave their gangs to join it. And second, I didn't know where to send them to find such a place.

Consider the definition of the Greek word for fellowship, *koinonea*, which is described in this passage. It literally means "to give, contribute, share; to be initiated into the mysteries of Christ; to participate in the deeds of others, being equally responsible for them." Embodied in the term *koinonea* is the core definition of a gang!

While the church does possess many of the essential things young offenders need, sadly, the worlds of at-risk teenagers and Christ-centered churches are usually at opposite ends of the spectrum. And, oftentimes, each has been sufficiently burned or turned off by the other that distrust abounds.

So how can the church best engage troubled youth, accepting them where they are, yet without compromising biblical standards? What is the best strategy for ministering to them? What kind of expectations should we have? Such questions form the substance of this chapter. But before we talk about a strategy of ministering to young offenders, we must first gain a clearer understanding of who they are, and who they are not.

Understanding Today's Juvenile Offender

Many well-meaning adults mistakenly assume that the term *urban youth* is synonymous with the term *at-risk youth*. While many urban communities do constitute a risk factor for kids, simply living in a particular zip code does not define a young person as being "troubled" or "at risk." This is a critical distinction for inner-city youth workers to understand. To be ignorant of this reality causes many difficulties.

For example, an urban church leadership council might naturally balk at the thought of reaching out to young offenders or gang-involved youth, reasoning, "Our kids here in the church are at risk. Why are we worrying about all those others outside of here, when we have so many needs among our own?"

Another understandable temptation of inner-city youth ministries is to seek public or private funding for outreach programs targeted to at-risk youth, when in reality they are sidestepping the "real problem kids" in favor of those teenagers who are least at risk—the ones who faithfully attend programs and pose no threat of being unruly or disruptive.

Don't misunderstand. There's nothing wrong with targeting such inner-city youth, but to mistakenly assume or report that a legitimate at-risk population is being reached is misleading. At-risk and troubled youth must be intentionally targeted, otherwise they will not naturally be reached. Why? Because they won't "just show up," and if they do, your first tendency might well be to ask them to not come back, particularly if their behavior is disruptive.

Yet, as Christian youth workers, we are called to minister to such young people in our communities. To effectively do so, we must first understand some of the common characteristics of most highly at-risk youth, particularly juvenile offenders.

Family Dysfunction

For many reasons, less than half of today's children are growing up living with their married, biological parents.[1] In fact, within some ethnic groups, up to 80 percent of children live in a mother-only family for at least part of their lives.[2] The statistics are much higher for juvenile offenders.

When Fathers are Missing

There have actually been periods of higher fatherlessness in our country than today, such as during times of war. But the death of a father is different from the abandonment of a father. When a father is unknown or lives only a few blocks away but has little or no interest in or contact with his child, as is the case with most juvenile offenders, several common traits emerge.

A Hatred for Authority—A hatred for authority is almost always prevalent in kids whose first authority figure is either absent or abusive. Consequently, when a teacher says "Sit down," they stand up. They hate the principal, the coach, and the police. They come to hate their boss at work, their probation officer—anyone who takes on the role of an authority figure in their lives.

When my wife, Hanne, and I began taking boys into our home as they were coming out of prison, I remember being confused. Why did they like me when I visited them in jail, but suddenly begin to dislike me once we took them into our home? I would sometimes ask if anything was wrong, or if I had offended them in some way.

They would say no. For even they didn't understand why their feelings toward me had changed. In time I began to realize that it's normal for a young person to subconsciously transfer the hatred they hold toward the role of a "father" onto anyone who begins to fill that role in his or her life. Victor, one of the boys who lived with us upon his release from lockup, expressed this philosophy quite well: "I've been hurt so many times that I'll hurt you before you have a chance to hurt me."

To affect real change in kids like Victor requires that somebody remains alongside them long enough to outlive that role of a negative authority figure until slowly but surely a new, more positive one is created in its place. This, in turn, opens such kids up to accepting other authorities that come into their lives...including God.

Deep-Seated Anger—Deep-seated anger is the second trait usually present in kids who grow up without a positive father figure. This is the dominant emotion of distressed and troubled teenagers.

I sometimes ask kids to imagine that they have an "anger thermometer" inside them which reads "0" when no anger is present, and "10" when they are over the edge and out of control.

"What does your thermometer read when you're not upset at anything in particular?" I ask. Most say it never goes below "7" or "8".

If someone looks at one of these young people angrily, or stares suspiciously at them when passing on the street, this might send them up two or three notches on an anger thermometer. No problem if a person is at "0" to begin with. But if they are already at "8," all of a sudden they're out of control, and somebody's going to get hurt.

When I ask kids in lockup how many of them committed their crimes when they were at "10," the majority raise their hands.

Where is all this anger coming from? It's been my experience that this type of deep-seated anger usually comes from being rejected by someone close to us, often in childhood, and most often a father. I remember asking a group of kids in a detention center Bible study how many of them had ever felt rejected as children. Five of the eleven told stories of how their fathers or stepfathers had tried to hurt or kill them when they were young.

If the root of the problem is *rejection*, then the solution must be *acceptance*. This is not just making the bland statement, "I accept you as you are," which is closer to apathy and indifference. But rather, we must extend the kind of acceptance that God extends toward us. He knows us at our worst yet loves us completely, enough to change us.

Lack of Identity—The role of a father is essential for a child's healthy sense of identity. For girls, fathers are tied to their sense of security and sexual identity. For boys, father figures are essential to teaching them what it is to be a man.

A Los Angeles Times Magazine cover story entitled "Mothers, Sons, and the Gangs: When a Gang Becomes Part of the Family" featured several single mothers who each lamented, "I don't understand why [my son] goes out on the streets. I'm a good mother. I keep a clean house, I go to church, I don't run around with men, I cook for the boy, wash his clothes, and provide a good home. Why doesn't he want to stay here?"[3] While a mother does many essential things, she cannot model for a boy how to be a man.

When Mothers Are Missing

Just as a child is damaged by a missing father figure, a missing mother has negative effects as well—perhaps even more so than with absentee fathers. We've had three boys live with us who were abandoned by their mothers as infants; each was far more damaged and maladjusted than any other kids who have lived with us who had been abandoned by their fathers.

When a mother abandons a child, the devastation is deep and profound, as she is the center of a child's life for the first two years. In fact, her absence is the cause of many "attachment disorders" that have become one of the more common diagnoses given to many of today's juvenile offenders. Maternal care and affection, especially in the early years of a child's life, are critical for a child to attach and form significant, bonding relationships later in life. Tragically, the crack cocaine epidemic of the 1980s did something in our inner cities that poverty and even slavery couldn't do. It separated mothers from their children. Many of these children are in our juvenile facilities today as teenagers.

Failure Complex

I once asked a group of kids at a detention center Bible study, "What would you like to be doing in five years?"

Luis spoke first. "I'll be in prison."

"Why do you say that?" I challenged him. "You'll be out of here in a couple of months."

"Cause I've always *been* a troublemaker and I'll always *be* a troublemaker."

I wondered how many times Luis had heard that said about him in his short life. Most at-risk youth like Luis have experienced so much failure in their young lives that they no longer believe they can succeed at anything. In fact, many of them begin to subtly feel more comfortable failing than they do succeeding. Success is scary. Failure is at least familiar.

Recently I reconnected with a boy who was back in the detention center where I had seen him many times over the past three years. "What happened?" I asked him.

"I don't know. I guess I was just doing *too* good," he responded. "I was back in school, I had a job, and things were really coming together. My family was proud of me for the first time I can remember. Then I just started getting scared. I knew I wouldn't be able to keep it up, and eventually I was going to crash and disappoint everybody, so I figured I might as well just screw up now, before I had too much to lose."

Failure complexes can run so deep. It's not surprising that one of the most common tattoos worn in adult prisons says simply, "Born to Lose."

Every young person needs to know there is a specific purpose for his or her life. That's why participation in service projects and opportunities to give to others are so essential for troubled young people. Tyrone expressed it well when he returned from one of our summer mission trips and told me, "I finally found the reason I was born." Now he had something bigger to say yes to than all the things we try to get such kids to say no to. Frankly, until this happens, most of our interactions with troubled teenagers are reduced to the level of "sin management."

Biblically Illiterate

The majority of kids who are locked up are a full two generations removed from anything remotely Christian. Fathers are usually out of the picture entirely, and most of the mothers possess but a distant memory of authentic faith. Typically a grandmother is the closest family link to vibrant Christianity.

Because of the spiritual void in so many youth, many have come to "spiritualize" their criminal activity. For example, one of the fastest growing sects in American prisons is the "Five Percent Nation," a radical, militant offshoot from the Nation of Islam. Another popular marriage of religion and criminality happens with "Sanatoria," a melding of voodoo superstition with Roman Catholicism that's popular among Hispanic youth.

The good news is that kids who are locked up are hungry for God and for spiritual answers. We find that between 35 and 40 percent of the population in a juvenile jail come to Bible study when it is offered to them. It also means that we need to be very basic in our teaching, as they likely won't know much about God or the Bible. But that can also make teaching the Bible exciting, as these kids don't already know the end of the story before you begin. They sit on the edge of their seats saying excitedly, "Then what happened?"

Emotionally Damaged

There are nearly 3 million arrests of juveniles in the United States each year. Similarly, there are about 3 million reported cases of abuse and neglect annually upon youth and children.[4] I don't know if they are all the same kids, but you can be sure that many are. In fact, experiencing abuse or neglect as a child is the number one indicator of future trouble with the law in the teenage years.

A recently released report on juvenile offenders in my home state of Massachusetts found that 44 percent had been stabbed or shot, 35 percent had personally witnessed another person being killed, and 40 percent met the diagnostic criteria for post-traumatic stress disorder.[5] These children have experienced more trauma by age sixteen than the average adult will encounter in an entire lifetime!

Fifteen-year-old José expressed this painful reality in the following prayer-request note he handed one of our detention Bible study leaders recently:

"Please pray for my friend Jared. He hung himself Sunday. I pray that he made it to heaven. Please pray my dad comes home from jail in thirty days and my HIV test comes back with what God wanted it to be."

Kids like José who have been damaged often exhibit many other destructive tendencies as well. Marijuana is perhaps the most popular form of medicating such pain. As one boy in detention put it, "Marijuana is Novocain for the soul."

We also know that whenever abuse, trauma, or heavy drug and alcohol use invade the life of a young person, emotional development comes to a halt.[6] Kids tend to remain stuck there emotionally, even though they continue developing physically. Thus, many troubled and at-risk high schoolers still struggle with issues that better-adjusted adolescents have resolved. As a result, issues of fairness, power, and respect, which are normally resolved in middle school, are still enormous for troubled kids in their late teen years and beyond.

In fact, today's adult prison environment remarkably parallels the culture of a middle-school playground where issues of respect, power, and pecking order abound. When ninety-five-pound kids struggle to figure out the pecking order on playgrounds, the result is a few bloody noses and an occasional black eye; when adults in two-hundred-pound bodies with weapons struggle to work their issues out, the results are much more tragic. There is no jungle quite like that of grown-ups living in a middle-school world.

The Need for Adults

Healthy adults are absolutely essential for at-risk teenagers to resolve these developmental issues. Thus, a church youth group is generally not the place to plug in such youth. One reason is that these kids have had far more life experience than the average youth group kid. Obviously, witnessing a homicide firsthand places a teenager in an entirely different category of life experience than the average adolescent, even if both have grown up in the same neighborhood.

Another reason traditional youth groups sometimes don't work well for these kids is that the at-risk guys pose an immediate threat to the boys in the youth group. Suddenly they now are in competition with each other for the youth group girls. And youth group girls tend to have a fascination with boys who are on the edge.

The remedy for young offenders is intense adult intervention like that described by the Apostle Paul in 1 Corinthians 4:15: "For though you may have countless guides in Christ, you do not have many fathers. But I became your father in Christ Jesus through the gospel" (RSV). These kids need to be re-parented, as I wrote about extensively in the book *At Risk: Bringing Hope to Hurting Teenagers* (Group Publishing, 1999).

At-risk teenagers tend to fit much better into young adult age groups, or into the church at large, than into youth groups. In such groups they are not a threat to one another, they have more in common when it comes to life experiences, and there are not as many potentially damaging boy-girl relationships to develop. I have also seen great success with "youth churches" targeted toward young men and women coming out of gangs like Jason and the other gang members I mentioned at the beginning of this chapter.

A youth church designed specifically for highly at-risk youth can also serve as sort of a "pre-church," where adults who lead the program come together with teenagers on less threatening ground. Then as relationships develop, and kids grow in their faith and maturity, the transition to the larger church body can more successfully take place.

Establishing an Effective Juvenile Justice Ministry

Below are several guiding principles for urban youth workers who desire to establish an effective ministry to juvenile offenders who are locked up in their communities.

Establish the Right Parameters

Juvenile institutional ministry happens in a completely different context than church youth ministry. Juvenile facilities are responsible for the youth in their care, and we are under their authority when we enter their facility. Some of the concerns treatment staff may have about religious programs are that kids might become sidetracked from dealing with their issues, something they often fear religion may do.

Treatment staff also worry about kids not taking ownership for their behavior, saying, "The devil made me do it." They're concerned kids may use God as a way to escape taking responsibility for their actions. Also, because these youth are minors, the potential argument over separation of church and state always exists. "People aren't allowed to come into public schools and lead Bible studies. Why should we allow it here?" they ask.

The short answer is because locked-up youth don't have access to religious services, and juvenile institutions have the responsibility for making such services available to their residents. If you're privileged to be the option that's offered, it's essential that certain guidelines are adhered to when you design your program.

Here are the primary issues that address treatment officials' legitimate concerns when launching a faith-based program in a juvenile facility:

· Voluntary—not a mandatory program for youth.

· Interdenominational—make sure it's available for all kids, and be careful to avoid controversial doctrines such as mode of baptism, spiritual gifts, and so on. Focus on the foundations of the gospel and don't cut down other denominations.

· Positive—not condemning.

· Consistent—meeting each week at the same time with the same leaders (ideally two), for a minimum of a one-year commitment.

When properly designed and administered, staff see such a program as an integral component of their overall treatment program for youth. In fact, some of the most fruitful ministry can occur with staff when an attitude of servanthood is displayed. Inviting staff to sit in on the Bible discussion group if they desire, or attending other events that the program offers, goes a long way. Also, make it a point to mention to them the positive things you see staff doing for the kids.

Because staff generally are very concerned for the best interest of the youth, if they see your program as contributing to that, they'll be much more inclined to encourage kids to attend.

Use Everyday Language

This is not suggesting that you try to use the kids' language and mannerisms. Nothing turns kids off quicker than an "old" person trying to be one of them. Be yourself.

What it does mean, however, is that we consciously attempt to use "non-Christianese" language. This is one of the hardest things for Bible study leaders to do. Terms like *salvation, justification, righteousness, holiness* mean absolutely nothing to most of these kids. Jesus didn't use big, sophisticated words. In fact, he usually told stories when he wanted to teach truths. Do the same.

Does that mean you shouldn't read the Bible, and only tell stories? Not at all. But it is important that you read from a version of the Bible that kids can understand. The Contemporary English Version, published by the American Bible Society and written at a third grade reading level, is one I highly recommend. Others to consider are The Living Bible, The Everyday Bible, New International Reader's Version, and The New Life Version.

Use a Discussion-Based Format

Rather than preaching or teaching, discussion-based sessions are most effective in juvenile facilities. The discussion format offers a much more relational approach and provides the best environment for both learning and nurturing. A good Bible study facilitator asks the right questions, leading kids to conclude the right answers.

The ideal setting is to have everyone to sit in a circle. That way, kids sense they are important contributors to the group, and that their input is valued.

The Bible discussion groups we facilitate in juvenile institutions work best for groups of two to twenty youth and last about an hour. The ground rules are few, but they are important:

1. Only one person speaks at a time.

2. Each person's opinion is respected.

3. No one in the group is allowed to talk about other staff or kids who aren't there.

The Bible studies we facilitate are topical, and they follow this basic format:

1. Opening discussion: Solicits general discussion on the topic in order to create a nonthreatening environment where it's clear that all input is welcome and appreciated. The questions should lead toward establishing a *question* or *problem* that is common to all. The goal is for the youth to conclude, "Yeah, this is an area of my life that I can't handle on my own" or "That's a question I've had for a long time, and I don't know the answer."

2. Story or illustration: This serves to further state the problem illustrated in the opening discussion. It helps create the need for a solution.

3. Scripture: Here is where the solution is introduced.

4. Wrap-up: This is where the leader transitions from an open discussion format into one of wrapping up the meeting. Be sure to reemphasize Scripture's answer to the problem/question introduced in the opening discussion. End by asking for prayer requests and praying.

It's important that the topics addressed are ones the kids are interested in or struggling with so we're not answering questions the kids aren't asking. We want to create a hunger in them for the truth, so that when we give the answer, it will fall on readied hearts.

Realize Where Your Power Comes From

America's prisons are the devil's backyard, and for anything eternal to happen, prayer is essential. When we began in 1987, God laid upon our hearts Nehemiah 4.16: Half the people did the work while half stood guard. Intercessory prayers are the ones who stand guard. We have three people pray for each institution's needs every day, with updated requests from the kids weekly. Countless miracles attest to the faithfulness of those prayers.

Some time ago I called the director of a detention center and asked if he would consider allowing us to hold a Bible study there. He said, "I don't want anybody coming in here telling these kids that Jesus Christ is God. Will your group be doing that?"

"There's a pretty good chance that we will," I said.

"Then I'm not interested," was his response.

That was about as flat a rejection as I had ever received. Still, I decided to send him some ministry information anyway, as well as to put it on our daily prayer chain. Several weeks later that same director called back, asking if there was any way we could start a Bible study at his unit. Prayer works!

Leave the Goods Behind

The first time we brought in a bag of Bibles and testimony books to a juvenile jail, you would have thought they were made of gold. Kids were lunging for them. Youth who are locked up have time on their hands and a great sense of need—two essential ingredients for spiritual growth. You may see them only one hour a week, but God can use the materials you leave with them to keep them growing in your absence.

Our organization, Straight Ahead Ministries, publishes testimony books, devotional books, and a ten-part discipleship book course that can be given to youth to read while they've got the time and motivation. We also publish books and training materials for those who are called to work with juvenile offenders. They can all be ordered through our Web site: www.straightahead.org.

Be Thinking Aftercare

The key—and most difficult—part of any juvenile offender ministry is solid aftercare. While many assume that mentoring is the way to go with such youth, it takes more than just a mentor to effectively follow up a high-risk youth who's returning to the inner city. There are so many negative factors awaiting teenagers as they re-enter the streets, that for a mentor to even find the kid in those first thirty days is a challenge.

And let's face it, most older adolescent offenders are not looking for a "big brother" or sister. That's why it's important to discern what the young person does want. A job? to get back into school? vocational skills? tutoring? to fulfill a community service requirement? a more positive environment to hang around? If you can figure out what he or she wants and connect together around that, mentoring does happen. But it happens as a byproduct and much more naturally.

Discipleship homes are another effective means of aftercare for juvenile offenders. Of the youth who have come through our homes, the recidivism rate is 10 percent, versus the national average of 75 percent for youth being re-arrested after release from juvenile institutions.

The Heart of Jesus

There is no more rewarding ministry than to have the opportunity to minister to young juvenile offenders. Throughout Scripture, God actively seeks out at least five types of people: the poor, the sick, the orphan, the widow, and the imprisoned. On any given day in a juvenile detention center, you'll likely meet three or four of these. If you want to be where God's heart is, what better place than in our juvenile jails? May his Spirit go before you and with you!

Endnotes

[1] Linda Nielsen, *Adolescence: A Contemporary View, Third Edition* (Fort Worth, TX: Harcourt Brace College Publishers, 1996), 350-351.

[2] Evelyn K. Moore, "The Call: Universal Child Care," *Building a 21st Century Community: The State of Black America 1996* (New York, NY: National Urban League), http://cgi.nul.org/soba96.html.

[3] Sue Horton, "Mothers, Sons, and the Gangs: When a Gang Becomes Part of the Family," Los Angeles Times Magazine, October 16, 1988, 8, quoted in Gordon Dalby, *Father and Son: The Wound, the Healing, the Call to Manhood* (Nashville, TN: Thomas Nelson, Inc., 1992), 32.

[4] Michael Petit and Thomas R. Brooks, "Abuse and Delinquency: Two Sides of the Same Coin," *Reclaiming Children and Youth* (Summer 1998), 77-79, quoted in Scott Larson and Larry Brendtro, *Reclaiming Our Prodigal Sons and Daughters* (Bloomington, IN: National Education Service, 2000), 94.

[5] Gleaned from an oral interview with Suzanne Jazzman, Clinical Director for the Massachusetts Department of Youth Services on November 5, 1999.

[6] Mary W. Armsworth and Margot Holaday, "The Effects of Psychological Trauma on Children and Adolescents," *Journal of Counseling and Development*, Volume 72 (September/October 1993), 49-56.

Chapter 11
Developing a Mentoring Ministry
Peter Vanacore

Steve stood me up the first time I went to meet him. That's pretty typical behavior for an urban teenager when a stranger from a mentoring program comes to visit. Most mentors will tell you that it takes time for the teenager to trust and like a mentor. In this case, Steve missed our meeting because he had a more pressing appointment: with a judge over a burglary charge. I eventually matched Steve with a volunteer mentor who nurtured him for the next ten years. Today Steve is a mature Christian adult being used by the Lord.

Throughout the ages young wise men have sought wiser, older men to advise them on life issues. King Odysseus sought a wise counselor for his young son Telemachus, according to Homer in the *Odyssey*. Odysseus chose Mentor, a man he valued, as the right person for the job.

Biblical examples include Moses and Joshua, Paul and Timothy, and most revealing, Jesus and his disciples. Throughout the Gospels we can see how Jesus invested time with them, bearing their weaknesses, strengthening their faith, and encouraging them toward God's call in their lives.

While some seek mentors, many of our youth are at best alienated and at worst completely separated from adults who can provide them much-needed help. They do not choose mentors on their own, either because they don't see the importance of such a relationship, or because they don't know of any adults who would take that much interest in them. Either way, many of these young men and women would respond enthusiastically, over time, to positive adult mentors.

Understanding the Issues

The need for mentors in urban areas is overwhelming. In some cities there are communities in which over 75 percent of the children are born to single mothers. For many, not only are the children born to single mothers; they tend to stay without fathers in the home for the rest of their lives.[1]

According to a Rutgers University study, "Today, single mothers are increasingly likely to have never married. And they are more likely to stay single, so unwed motherhood has become a permanent status for many women."[2]

Many studies have shown that fatherless young men are more likely to become troubled. Young girls also need female mentors. Many females, especially in our cities, grow up without mothers or with mothers who are so weighed down with their own life issues that they have little time, energy, or sometimes ability to invest in their daughters. Numerous studies have shown that among young people who live in single-parent households or households where both parents work, drug and alcohol use is higher.

According to a government study of mentoring programs, quality mentoring programs directly address risk factors for today's youth, concluding: "The very presence of a mentor in a youth's life can help to reduce isolation and provide needed supervision and support."[3]

I matched my first teenager with a mentor in the early 1980s. Kenyon, a young, strapping fifteen-year-old with a criminal record long enough to match his attitude, began to meet weekly with Steve, a thirty-something guy with an equally colorful past. Kenyon's probation officer encouraged, but did not require, that Kenyon become involved in a mentoring relationship. Little did I know that Kenyon was a member of a radical Islamic cult known as the Five Percent Nation of Islam that preached of self-deification and hatred of all those who did not accept their way of life.

Two turbulent years later, Kenyon gave his life to Jesus and started to regularly attend a church in his community. He didn't fit the choirboy description, but everyone who knew Kenyon began to see his life slowly transform. The cult was part of his past, and a new life emerged as God used him in the lives of many people.

Kenyon was already troubled when Steve entered his life. Steve provided a male voice to a confused youth who thought all males were destined for irresponsibility. Steve met with him because he cared, which gave this young man a sense of worth that he never previously possessed. This relationship could never replace a relationship with a father, but it did provide a model of God-directed masculinity.

The Case for Mentoring

The National Mentoring Institute sought the opinions of a group of street teenagers in Boston to find out what they needed or respected in adults. Here are some of the key qualities they said they look for in adults: the ability to get past obstacles, consistency, commitment, understanding, and the ability to listen.[4] Teenagers want people who will accept them for who they are but challenge them for who they could be.

Why Mentor?

We can best see what type of person makes the best mentor by first examining some possible motivations for involvement.

I'm gonna change that kid. This is the most common motivation I see for people who want to mentor. Some Christians want a notch on their Bibles for saving lost teenagers; others seek the praise that may come from others for their noble efforts. Overall, this is a motivation that can do damage because the mentor is seeking to fill God's role in redemption and take the credit. We may be vehicles of God's grace, but only God can transform.

God will change this kid through me. We don't know what God is going to do. People are resistant to change even when they know it will make their lives better. God can change anyone, but people must be willing to welcome God's work in their lives. When a street kid comes to Jesus, his spirit may be willing, but his flesh is very weak. True transformation, that incorporates all areas of life, takes years of seeking God through his Word, prayer, and the sharpening fellowship of the Church. A street kid with Jesus is still a street kid until he is nurtured into a new way of life. Mentors who expect a young person to instantly change will usually become discouraged and abandon their efforts along with the teenager.

All they need is a little love. They need a lot of love, and they will test anyone claiming to love them to make sure that love is real. Many teenagers are so accustomed to abandonment that they reason, as one young man said to his mentor, "I'd feel more comfortable if you beat me than love me."

In 1 Corinthians 13, Paul describes the type of love needed to reach out to a needy teenager: "[Love] always protects, always trusts, always hopes, always perseveres" (1 Corinthians 13:7). Mentors need to bear with teenagers that most people think are unbearable. They must believe in the teenagers and cling to the solid hope that God can reach a young person many may think is unreachable.

Most of all, a mentor must endure through times when discouragement would tempt the mentor to quit. Other Christians or family members may ask, "Why are you wasting your time with that ungrateful kid?" Yet faith, hope, and love must see them through the trials.

I will remain faithful. Paul continues his thoughts in I Corinthians 13 by saying, "Love never fails." Love cannot fail if it is given without any expectation of reciprocation. This type of unconditional love holds people to be faithful in their commitments to mentor teenagers, even when they see no signs of hope. Volunteer mentors who endure through the most difficult times always see the fruit of their labor in their own lives, and often they stay long enough to see the fruit take hold in a young person's life as well. I have seen mentors keep relationships with teenagers for five, ten, and even more years. A seemingly hopeless boy at fourteen years of age can be a joyful young man at twenty-four years through the transforming power of the Holy Spirit and the nurture of committed Christians.

I will be real. Mentors who are comfortable with themselves—not needing pretentious facades of superiority or spirituality—are able to let teenagers see them as forgiven sinners. They are in as desperate need of God's touch as anyone else. This security leads them to ask for forgiveness when they make mistakes. Criticism from young people is seen as faithful wounds from friends. They are also able to bear with the weaknesses of their young friends because they understand their own weaknesses and frailty.

Mentoring Myths

For almost two decades, a diverse range of American leaders has touted mentoring as the cure for a myriad of youth problems. The results of mentoring often have not lived up to the hype. Following are some myths about mentoring, along with common-sense responses.

Every kid wants a mentor. The logic goes that teenagers are starving for adult attention. And because so many boys grow up without a consistent male figure in the home and most intact families have two working parents, almost any teenager will want the adult attention that mentoring provides. The truth is that while many teenagers *need* mentors, not all of them *want* one. They like being with their friends much more than with adults.

Despite this reticence to becoming involved with adults, matching the right teenager with the right adult can work miracles. Adolescents have misconceptions of adults, just as most adults misunderstand teenagers. A good mentor meeting with a teenager who has even just a dim spark of interest can build a healing relationship that can last a lifetime.

Mentoring is an inexpensive way to reach youth. That's true, but only if you compare it to residential ministry. On a per-person basis, running a mentoring ministry is one of the most expensive ways to reach youth. Even if you are running a small program in your church, there is a significant investment in time and resources to make the mentoring relationships work. It is much more cost effective to preach or run Bible studies. Yet while those ministries are great at spreading God's Word, mentoring can build upon such efforts by making disciples. I have yet to meet a mature Christian who didn't have at least one solid believer who invested some quality and quantity time in him or her. Mentoring provides a forum for that to happen.

Pedophiles make mentoring too high-risk. These people are rare. In all my years of ministry, I believe I had only one try to become a volunteer. Yet one can ravage a young person's life and destroy a ministry's reputation. Thorough screening and consistent supervision are the only ways to protect the youth God has entrusted to your care.

There are not enough mentors for urban youth. It takes work to find good mentors in any community, but every community has various sources of Christian adults who have the ability and resources to make this kind of commitment. The keys are finding and motivating them. It is helpful, of course, to have indigenous people recruit for their own communities because they have grass-roots connections that motivate individuals to service. If you are just beginning your program or are planning for a small number of mentors, your own connections with local people will work best. Sometimes you can even find a volunteer recruiter who has deeper community connections and can help champion your recruiting efforts.

Cross-cultural mentoring relationships don't work. This is a growing perception among some groups of Christians. Yet those of us who work in mentoring ministries have not found it to be true. These relationships provide benefits for both teenagers and adults because everyone learns more thoroughly how to appreciate and communicate with other cultures. The keys are willingness on both parts to reach out cross-culturally, along with a desire and ability on the mentor's part to learn and grow. A mentor must be able to confront his or her own misconceptions or prejudices in order to make this type of relationship work. When that happens, the teenager is much more willing to make the same journey.

Developing an Effective Mentoring Program

Every youth minister mentors teenagers informally because mentoring becomes a natural part of life. You hang out with teenagers, play ball with them, fix your car together, or help them find a job or pick a college. They look to you as a trusted friend and advisor, while you labor to see their faith take strong root. Neither of you may call it mentoring, but that's what you're doing. It's a friendship that benefits everyone.

Formal mentoring programs link teenagers and adults with no prior relationships and seek to build friendships between strangers. Think about the awkwardness of this. You're putting together people who don't know each other, who are unsure if they like each other, and asking them to build long-term relationships. It has the same sort of feel as an arranged marriage. In some cases you may ask them to sign an informal agreement stating their commitment to build friendships. How can this possibly work? It works when you implement the following four main elements of a successful program.

Keys to Success

Successful mentoring programs across the country universally recognize the first three keys to success. Screening, training, and supervision are the bedrock components to ensure quality, effective mentoring.[5] The fourth element, prayer, adds a dimension of support and power that will help teenagers truly thrive.

Screening

Screening is essential for both adults and youth to determine their suitability for mentoring relationships. The first part of your screening actually begins with the recruiting of mentors. How and where you recruit will most likely determine the type of people who apply.

If you put an ad in a local newspaper, you will need to screen through many inappropriate people in a time-consuming and often frustrating process of filtering them down to a few good people. Secular programs, such as Big Brothers Big Sisters, do this because they have a broad mission that allows volunteers of any faith to participate. Their advertising not only recruits volunteers; it also serves a public-relations function that raises their community profile, which helps in fundraising. Targeting a church or Christian group narrows your potential pool, but also provides a more focused group of potential volunteers.

The way you present the mentoring ministry to the church will also affect your screening process. I once gave a short recruiting presentation during a Sunday morning service that produced a large outpouring of volunteers because I told emotional stories of hurting teenagers in their community who needed and wanted their friendship. Most of those volunteers did not pan out. I learned that realistic presentations that gave not only the hope, but also the reality of building relationships with troubled youth, produced volunteers who understood the level of commitment involved in mentoring. This made the screening process much less time consuming. I eventually learned that the stories I told helped determine even the gender of the people who responded. Emotional stories that emphasized the teenagers' families attracted more women, while stories of fun and exciting activities that helped change teenagers' lives attracted more men.

Screening also involves having volunteers fill out applications and seeking references from key people such as the applicants' pastors, employers, closest friends and spouses or closest family members. The references from family members provide key information about people's character and whether spouses are equally committed to their wives or husbands spending time with teenagers. Many mentoring relationships end because spouses resent the time taken away from the home.

Police background checks can be a double-edged sword. They scare off people who may be dangerous with teenagers, but they also may keep away people who have been transformed by the Lord after a criminal past. Most of these checks are limited to any criminal history in one's own state of residence only and not in other parts of the country. Yet they are often required by insurance companies or even state authorities. You can contact your local police department or juvenile justice agency for help in obtaining this information. Sometimes a motor vehicle background check will reveal more about a person's character than a criminal background check because it reveals how responsible people are with a crucial area of their lives. You don't want a reckless driver taking your kid out for a Saturday cruise. These checks are available through the state motor vehicle department.

The teenagers also need screening. Do they really want to be in the program, or are parents or other adult authorities forcing them? What are their interests, their likes and dislikes? What are their personality profiles, and with what kinds of adults would they mesh? What do they expect from the relationship? Do their parents or guardians want the relationships, and what do they expect? Answering these questions will help you discern whether the teenager is a good fit for one of your mentors.

Training

Intertwined in the screening process is the orientation and training of new potential mentors. An interactive orientation for prospective volunteers serves several purposes. First, it gives you an opportunity to observe people as they interact with the other prospects. Discussions, role-plays, and just socializing over coffee give you some hints into the interpersonal skills of each person. Are they comfortable with new people? Do they listen well, or do they dominate conversations?

Second, the orientation gives volunteers the opportunity to understand the basics of the ministry and the expected commitment. Before making a commitment to teenagers, volunteers should know what they are getting into. The last thing that should happen is for volunteers to come back to you after they're matched with youth and say, "This is not what I agreed to!"

The orientation should present, as realistically as possible, what people should expect from the mentoring relationships and the ministry. Of course the vicissitudes of human life make behavioral predictions more of an art form than a science. Many mentors state that while they understood the commitment in theory, they had no idea of the emotional energy involved in developing relationships with needy teenagers. Problems and crises of all sorts are regular occurrences for many of our teenagers who live on the fringes of mainstream society.

The last benefit of the orientation is that even if a person decides not to volunteer, the education he or she receives from the program can motivate the person to add to your program in other key ways. Many people who cannot make the commitment or do not feel called to mentor can still provide other types of assistance such as office help, phone calls, or help with retreats and activities. Even if that is not possible, if they leave the training feeling positive about the ministry, they may promote your program to other people or provide financial support.

Everyone should leave an orientation with four questions answered: What should I expect from my relationship with the teenager? How will the ministry help me in the relationship? How can I start to build a friendship with my match? Are there any other ways I can help this ministry reach teenagers?

Ongoing training during the mentor relationship helps to support volunteers and provides insight on building closer relationships with their matches. Whereas an orientation prepares volunteers for the relationships, once involved in the successes and struggles of those relationships, volunteers are usually more able and willing to learn.

Supervision

This is the area that makes or breaks mentoring. The quality of the supervision of the mentoring relationships will most likely determine whether those relationships produce enduring fruit in teenagers' lives. Good mentoring programs that see long-term results spend at least as much effort and resources in the supervision as they do in the recruiting and screening. This is what makes mentoring a costly ministry. If you had to just match them and set them loose, the ministry would be easy.

The problem is that without the help of wise supervisors, who act almost as caseworkers, most of the mentoring relationships will fail. And a failed relationship only reinforces the negative feelings many youth already have about adults and themselves.

Adult mentors often face a minefield of problems that are beyond their experience and capacity to handle without outside help. Family, education, legal, and peer problems can easily overwhelm the average churchgoer. Compounding this are the typical struggles of trying to build a relationship with a teenager who is going through the normal, tumultuous stages of adolescent development. Without the support of a trained adviser, even the most committed volunteer can give up on the relationship—often without giving it a full chance to get started.

Long Island Youth Guidance in New York provides one of the best examples of mentor supervision of any program I know of, whether Christian or secular. They have well-trained, devoted staff who work with the mentors and the teenagers' families to insure that the relationships will endure and produce results. Their staff calls or visits the volunteers and teenagers to make sure they are meeting regularly and the relationships are going well. They provide advice and support for the volunteers to help them work through difficult relational issues and set goals to make the relationships more fruitful. The staff interfaces with the teenagers' families and often works alongside schools, social service agencies, and juvenile justice officials to provide a holistic range of ministry.

Contact with the teenagers' families—and often ministry to them—is essential, especially with young teenagers and pre-teenagers. Most teenagers in need of mentors have families with many needs as well. Churches need to come alongside these families to bring the love of Christ, along with some practical resources. If you ignore the family, the match often dies because the family inevitably begins to interfere with the relationship. The mentor cannot do all of this type of ministry as it can be very overwhelming, and it takes away from the primary relationship with the teenager.

Admittedly, most of us are not able to provide this level of investment into mentoring. The alternative is to start small inside a church or organization with a trusted group of mentors who can be easily supervised. Work with those adults to find and screen your next batch of mentors. You probably already know the teenagers who need to be matched. Always start small until you learn your capabilities. You can always grow as momentum develops. Although some youth pastors are gifted supervisors and administrators, a volunteer from a human service field can provide the same support, freeing the youth leader to concentrate on other areas of ministry.

Prayer

We know that prayer is the key element to everything that happens in life, yet we often neglect it. Mentors who work with high-risk teenagers in urban areas enter into a spiritual battleground that will test faith and endurance in ways they have not often previously experienced. They need the support of prayerful people committed to daily lifting them and the teenagers before the Lord in consistent, dedicated prayer. In our work with juvenile offenders at Straight Ahead Ministries, we consider this so important that we have a staff person whose sole duty is to coordinate prayer between the volunteers and a small army of prayer warriors. Some of Straight Ahead's affiliate programs find a prayer coordinator as one of their first volunteer or staff positions. Leaving out prayer is just as neglectful to the mentors and teenagers as omitting any of the other key components.

Building a Relationship

Most youth leaders know intuitively how to build a relationship with a teenager, but many lay mentors will need some help. The primary focus needs to be on building a trusting relationship. Activities that build common, shared experiences are a key element for any relationship. This is why it is imperative to match people with at least a few common interests. Some adults are more willing to explore teenagers' interest areas, and some teenagers may want to learn about the mentors' areas of expertise. Yet they need to have at least some core interests in common.

Sports are a drawing card for many teenagers of both genders, but they can usually enjoy sports with their friends. Adults can enter into their world if they have some level of expertise they can share with teenagers, or if they're both just willing to learn something new. Skills with cars, cooking, or any other practical area will draw other types of teenagers. Relationships can often focus on needs teenagers have that can be met through the adults. Tutoring or developing a job skill can not only help in very practical ways, but these activities can also work to cement a relationship between two new friends.

Discipleship should be a key ingredient of mentoring. Mentors with willing teenagers can take fifteen minutes to a half hour of their time together to study the Bible and pray. This should not be forced on a young person, and usually this requires some time of building trust first. Mentors may also take teenagers to church and introduce them to Christian peers.

The main focus in matching mentors with teenagers should be on the relationships. If the only benefit teenagers garnish from the relationships is knowing there are adults who understand and care for them, then in many cases a great deal has been accomplished. Teenagers who feel they have advocates in an uncaring world can have more confidence in facing its perils.

Still, some people need more structure to enter into mentoring relationships. Sit down with mentors beforehand and work on schedules that you think the teenagers and the adults can do together. In time mentors will find their own ideas and their own ways to build a friendship. I had one match that worked on restoring furniture, and another match between an older woman and a younger teenager who just got together to bake cookies. A helpful role you can play is to encourage them to be creative by suggesting interesting things to do together.

Undoubtedly, younger teenagers find it easier to bond with mentors than do older teenagers. A key time is before they turn fourteen years old because they are somewhat more open to adult influences. Older teenagers are sometimes willing to meet with mentors if they see particular needs in their lives or if they have trouble relating to teenagers in their community.

Additional Resources

There are many resources available on mentoring. Christian ministries such as Long Island Youth Guidance have years of experience and all the resources you need to start successful mentoring on a small or large scale. Group Publishing provides a mentoring curriculum, *Successful Youth Mentoring*, which provides twenty-four sessions for interaction between adults and teenagers. Straight Ahead Ministries has expertise in working with juvenile offenders. Secular programs such as Big Brothers Big Sisters have practical resources for your community, while The Mentoring Center can lead you to many other programs and materials. Other good resources are The National Mentoring Partnership, Friends of the Children, the California Mentor Foundation, Metro Denver Partners, and Kinship of Greater Minneapolis.

Just get started. God will direct you as you begin to take steps in faith.

Endnotes

[1] U.S. Department of Health and Human Services, National Vital Statistics Reports, Volume 47, Number 25, October 1999, page 16.

[2] David Popenoe and Barbara Dafoe Whitehead, "The State of Our Unions: The Social Health of Marriage in America" (The National Marriage Project, Rutgers University, 1999), 7. http://marriage.rutgers.edu/SOOU.htm.

[3] Shay Bilchik, Administrator, "Juvenile Mentoring Program 1998 Report to Congress" (U.S. Department of Justice, Office of Juvenile Justice and Delinquency Prevention, 1998), 6.

[4] James Becker, *Mentoring High-Risk Teenagers* (Center City, MN: Hazelden Foundation, 1994), 38.

[5] Cynthia L. Sipe, *Mentoring: A Synthesis of P/PV's Research: 1988-1995* (Philadelphia, PA: Public/Private Ventures), 9.

Chapter 12
Equipping Urban Churches to Enfold Troubled Teenagers

Rev. Claire Sullivan

Last year, while making a visit at a homeless respite care facility, my eye caught the attention of a tender-faced man having a cigarette. I was visiting another homeless guy sitting at the patio table, but I intentionally let this gentle-looking soul overhear our conversation and then slowly drew him into it. In the context of the conversation I discovered he needed pants—big pants.

When I brought the pants the next day, he was surprised I hadn't blown him off. He made a comment that people don't usually follow through on what they say they're going to do. The homeless man sitting next to him said, "Claire wouldn't forget you." He asked if he could talk to me, so we went into the chapel and he began to tell his story.

Jimmy was sixty-two years old and had grown up in the suburbs on the South Shore of Massachusetts in an upper-middle-class community. His brothers were all jocks and he was not. His father battered his sister and mother, and Jimmy always stood between his sister and father to take the beating.

At the age of sixteen, Jimmy and his friends were at an amusement park and stole several items valued at around fifty cents each. They were all busted and taken to the police station. A juvenile defender came to represent Jimmy and told him to admit he was guilty and he would only have to do community service.

Jimmy and his buddies all faced the judge together. But there was one difference. Jimmy's friends all had their fathers by their side, and he didn't. The judge remarked that Jimmy's life must not be worth much if even his own father didn't care enough to be there that day.

The judge sent Jimmy away for one year, while dismissing all the others.

Jimmy's spirit was crushed that day in the courtroom. I could hear it in his voice as he told it out loud for the first time. He would spend the next thirty years in and out of prison and detox centers while living a life of racketeering, alcoholism, drug addiction, dealing, and eventually abandoning a marriage of more than twenty-five years.

After working with homeless men and women for more than eleven years, I have concluded that almost every homeless adult has experienced a traumatic childhood or adolescence. In the same way, without Christ and the support of a Christian community, many at-risk teenagers will end up on the streets as homeless adults.

That day, at the age of sixty-two, Jimmy needed hope. But he also needed a pair of pants, new socks, and some clean shirts; and he needed to tell his story. He needed someone to sit and listen and give him full eye contact and attention; and he needed prayer. But more importantly, at the age of sixteen Jimmy had needed a father, a father figure, or a mentor to sit with him in court that day. It would have changed his future.

As the church and our communities are faced with the challenge of working with at-risk youth, gang members, the homeless, and the marginalized, we often look for something new and innovative. But the answer isn't really all that complicated. It doesn't take huge amounts of money, a sexy new title or model, a seminary education, or a course in Street Slang 101.

Jesus is the answer, and he illustrated the model. He hung out at a well and talked about water with a woman who could relate. He hung around a pool and asked a self-centered man full of self-pity if he really wanted to be whole. He sat around a dinner table of sinners and got to know them, ate what they ate, and even laughed with them.

He was a "church boy" who grew up in a religious family that did all the right things, and yet he was able to build relationships across culture, age, and gender. He dialogued with pagans without feeling his own faith threatened, because he knew who he was. Jesus went where the people were, built relationships with them, and gave them hope—the hope of eternal life.

We, the church, have that same call: to bring Christ to those who desperately need him. The method is simple, but it takes everything we have. The church is and has the answer. But how do we bring the world of our churches to bear on the lives of troubled young people on our urban streets?

Stacey

Stacey showed up at our outreach site on the Boston Common. She was a sarcastic, vulgar, hostile, and downright nasty seventeen-year-old. Stacey was also a magnet for trouble, constantly surrounded by young men involved in gangs and other illicit activities. While we led praise and worship on the streets, she and her pals would mock us, swear at us, and be as disruptive as possible.

One night one of her friends overheard a message being preached and came in to listen. Stacey tried to distract him and get him out of the prayer circle, but he shrugged her off and stayed for prayer. At the end of the night, as our outreach van was heading out, I became aware of the little girl in her eyes that looked so fragile and vulnerable. I went over and asked if she wanted me to take her somewhere. She made it clear she did not want our assistance.

As the weeks went by, I continued to seek out Stacey and she began to respond. She told me her mother had died when she was twelve years old and that her father was in prison; a battering and drug-dealing sister was incarcerated, and Stacey had been in foster care for the past five years. She was currently in the custody of her twenty-two-year-old brother from whom she was displaying bruises.

One evening at our outreach site the atmosphere became really hostile. Stacey came over to me, and I asked her if she would like to go into a shelter for the night. To my surprise, she said yes. When we arrived at the shelter she was turned away because she was not yet eighteen years of age. Suddenly I had to choose between leaving her on the streets or taking her to my house. I took her home.

We sat up and ate peanut butter and jelly sandwiches and Oreo cookies, drank milk, and talked about prostitution, her mother's death, my story growing up, and Jesus. We listened attentively to each other. She snuggled on the warm couch as I told her good night and prayed for her. We sat up many nights talking in my apartment after that. She began to introduce me to her friends as her mother, and calling me "Mama." Some nights she showed up and some nights she didn't.

One night at our outreach site she came up to me in a state of panic. She grabbed my arm and said, "Claire, I did something today that I told you I would never do. I prostituted." She sobbed and sobbed. I had a huge lump in my throat as I held her. I told her how sorry I was that she had experienced such a violation to her body, and she cried some more.

When Stacey turned eighteen, we threw a party for her outside the van. I asked her to come down to my office the next day. When I got to work that day she was already there. I told her I was giving her a gift that I thought my own mother would have given to me on my eighteenth birthday—a birthstone ring. She was grateful and overwhelmed; she asked me, "What's in that bottle on your desk?"

"It's anointing oil," I said, and I gave her a little two-minute teaching on the healing power of Jesus. "Can you put some of that on my head and pray for me?" she eagerly asked.

Stacey continues to come in and out of my life. She ended up pregnant, lost the baby, did time in prison, and continues in abusive relationships. She recently showed up at my office with her friend. I had not seen her in about a year. They wore platform shoes and glittery clothes, and had been turning tricks in Chinatown.

I said things like "Do you have any dreams? What are they? How's your sister? I'm so sorry about the loss of your baby. I want you to know I'm here."

Her friend started to join in. She shared that her grandmother brought her up in a Boston church and she had been to the church I used to attend. The room was becoming sweet with the Holy Spirit's hovering, comfort, conviction, and love. Both girls were beginning to feel convicted and unclean about their lifestyle, yet accepted and loved. I asked how they would feel if we prayed. They eagerly nodded yes. As I prayed for their protection and cleansing, I saw tears start to drop on the carpet. Afterward Stacey's friend said, "I feel so much better, so much cleaner than before I came in." I gave them my number, hugged them, and told them I loved them as they left.

What Is the Church?

How do we integrate teenagers like Stacey and her friend into the church? I guess that first depends on your definition of church. If your definition consists only of a building with pews, an altar, a choir, a pulpit, a deacon board, an education department, a nursery, and Sunday morning classrooms, there isn't much hope for teenagers like Stacey and her friends who are living on the streets.

But if church is coming together in community to seek God, to know him, to worship him, to give him thanks, to confess our sins, and to experience Christ's forgiveness and presence—and if church is a place to learn to grow in our faith together—then church can happen anytime and anyplace. "Church" ought to be more about an experience with God and with one another and less about a place.

Many of the homeless youth and adults in Boston will tell you they have a church. They'll describe it as an outreach van on Tuesday, Wednesday, and Thursday nights. It's the place where they receive a meal, clothing, and blankets for the night. It's the place where someone listens to their stories of the week and shares their burdens.

Richie and Laura, seventeen and nineteen years of age, are one couple I have had the privilege of getting to know. Richie had been using Ecstasy and a number of other drugs; his girlfriend Laura was pregnant. He wanted to clean up his act and take responsibility, knowing he soon would be a father.

They began attending our Tuesday night church service on the streets. Our team began to enfold them into their lives by forming a community around them. We put out the word that there was a need for baby items. Soon we had a number of baby items, including a baby stroller. Two of our outreach workers organized a small baby shower for them.

Richie's image of church is not what many mainstream Christians think of, but it is a place where he and his girlfriend experience church—on the sidewalks of Boston. It's where they live. And even though it's a dangerous place most evenings, every Tuesday night it becomes holy ground. God's presence comes alive in a community of people who seek him out. Church can be having breakfast in a booth at McDonald's with a homeless teenager. It can be in a juvenile jail rec room where a weekly Bible study happens.

Am I saying there's no need or place for the traditional church to enfold high-risk youth into their body? Not at all. In fact, I have never seen a person grow to deep maturity in Christ apart from a vital connection to a local church body. What I have been describing thus far may be better termed as a "pre-church" or a "bridge." It's taking the church to the streets where teenagers are and exposing them to the life-changing truths of Jesus as lived out in the community of his people in such a way that they're open to more fully stepping into that larger community of a church family.

Making a Bridge to the Church

Perhaps the best way to explain this process is through a story. Imagine that your church wants to build a bridge between themselves and the park next door. In addition to children who play there, there's also a gang of older teenagers who hang out there and play basketball. One of the teenagers, Josiah, has mouthed off a number of times to Mike, who is a member of your church.

Rather than trying to get Josiah and his crew banned from the park, suppose Mike walks over and respectfully hands Josiah a hammer and says, "Would you mind helping us on our construction team? We could really use another set of hands as we're trying to renovate this park."

Surprised by the invitation, Josiah agrees and starts hammering away. Carpentry being completely foreign to him, Josiah makes a lot of mistakes and has to start over many times. Rather than ridiculing him, Mike tells stories of how many times he screwed up building his first bridge. Soon Josiah's shame dissipates and his fear of failure begins to subside. While Josiah's first instinct is to swear every time he hits his finger with the hammer, he soon observes that none of the other men are being vulgar. As a result, he starts feeling a little convicted about his mouth and even begins to say, "Excuse me" when he slips.

Soon the crude form of a bridge takes shape. Josiah accepts an invitation to go with the guys to KFC for lunch. He sits and listens. The guys then ask him about his story. "How long have you lived in this neighborhood? Do you have brothers or sisters? Do you attend a school? What are some of your hopes and dreams?"

Slowly but surely Josiah is being integrated into a community of Christian men and beginning the transition into the family of God. You wouldn't put it in those terms, or he would feel manipulated, like *he's* the project rather than the bridge, but the sense of belonging and usefulness Josiah is experiencing is like nothing he has ever known.

Josiah is not invited into the church yet, but he is invited to a home-fellowship group that one of the men leads. Obviously, they don't tell him it's a "home-fellowship group" as such a description would certainly make him run. They just tell him it's a men's group. He attends one Thursday night and sees two other men from his construction team. Suddenly he feels like he belongs, has purpose, and is known. He hears men pray, confess sin, and weep. He feels the presence of God there—it feels safe.

Now it's the last week of the building project, and soon the bridge will be complete. Josiah is now standing at the door of the church with the other members of his team. He looks out at the bridge and sees some of his buddies from the park come over to check out the bridge. At first they heckle him, but then they linger to watch as the team puts on the finishing touches. Josiah feels proud of the skills he has mastered as he admires what he and the others were able to accomplish.

Once the project is over, Josiah misses working every week with his team. He can't put it into words, but it has to do with belonging to a family. These men have become like brothers to him. Mike has become like the father he never had. He's personally felt the power of Christ in his times with them. He's not willing to just let it end as a building project—Josiah wants more.

Obviously, I have painted an ideal picture. Most of us who work with troubled youth scarcely experience such a smooth transition. We see far more failures than successes. Nevertheless, I have described several key principles that work with young men and women from the streets as we try to help them successfully transition into a local church:

1. Start by going. Meet teenagers first in their community, whether it's in an institution or on the streets. Stay committed to them even if they want nothing to do with God. Our motivation is love, not manipulating people to Christ.

2. Begin working with one person and develop a relationship by listening to their stories of survival. Become a student of those you serve, allowing them to educate you and make you a better minister.

3. Find a ministry that's already doing what you want to do, and learn from their successes and failures. You don't have to make every mistake firsthand.

4. Be consistent. Build sacrifice into your schedule. Stay committed to the process no matter how many times you are blown off, insulted, or raged at. As we build mutual respect we can begin asking the hard questions and speaking correction, but not until we have built trust.

5. Realize that this is a long-term process with no set time frame for relationship building, transition, integration, or reconciliation. Stay in there for the long haul.

6. Look for the gifts and talents God has given them and affirm those gifts as they pop up. Don't just focus on all the negative stuff, but look for the hidden treasure and bless it. Allow teenagers to serve right where they are, whether that's helping out in the Bible study, setting up chairs, or helping out at an outreach site. That sense of purpose and ownership can provide the impetus they need to change their behavior.

7. Begin steps of transition by inviting the young person into your life through such things as a small group at church, a meal out, a ball game, or

whatever common ground you have to build on.

8. Allow the Holy Spirit to reveal what is in your heart through this relationship. Tough relationships bring up tough issues in our hearts. The relationship may trigger your own issues of brokenness and sin. Let the Holy Spirit heal and cleanse you in the process.

9. Model Christ before you try to present Christ. Create the experience of church through fellowship and love in preparation for bringing them into a formal church environment.

10. Help people in local churches to allow teenagers to find their place in the kingdom where they are, not where they're supposed to be, so they can move down the path to wholeness.

Hidden Treasures

Homeless and hurting teenagers are one of the greatest treasures any church can have. Not only are the lives of troubled young people transformed, but ours are as well, as we dare to take the church where Christ did—to those who are waiting to be found.

Chapter 13
The Urban Youth Church

Chris Hill

I love the church.

I was seven months old when my mother gave her life to Christ in a small inner-city Boston storefront church. It was the kind of church that had something going on six nights a week. I've attended Sunday School, youth camps and retreats, lock-ins, all-night bowling parties, street outreaches, and short-term mission trips. I've recited hundreds of Easter poems, played every role in youth group skits and plays, and ushered at hundreds of youth services. I've never missed a New Year's Eve service as long as I have been alive.

I love the church.

I realize, however, that I am a remnant of a dying breed. More and more young people today love God but hate the church. The very term "organized religion" has become a curse word to many. And vast numbers of youth have grown tired of the pomp and pageantry of the church, walking away, feeling sickened by its traditions.

Even many faithful brothers and sisters who labor evangelistically in parachurch organizations and outreach ministries have grown distant from the church. I am horrified by how few of them are even active members of local churches. For while they win young people to and through their organizational meetings, many have failed to connect them to local churches mostly because they themselves have grown distant from the church and our need for it.

This is understandable, for many of them were not won to Christ through local churches, but by street workers or parachurch ministries. With no personal context or history from which to draw, they simply repeat the cycle.

This is why I so firmly believe that we must lead today's urban youth to Christ *and* to his church, where they can find the necessary support and succor essential for them to grow into mature Christian adults.

But how? This process begins with us who serve in inner-city churches going out of our way to reach and retain the young people that our parachurch evangelists are winning to Christ. And it begins with those in parachurches partnering and building bridges with local churches so that both might win and disciple those in our inner cities to Jesus. Pastors need evangelists like fishermen need nets. One catches and the other keeps, but they have need of one another. Granted, it's easier said than done.

The Urban Situation

Having served as a youth pastor and youth evangelist for seventeen years, one of my greatest frustrations has been watching today's urban youth leave the church in droves. After years of sitting with sorrowful and sad parents of all races and cultures as they lamented the loss of their children's interest and passion for the things of God, I began to earnestly seek the Lord for solutions.

I began to pray, contemplate, and develop—alongside several trusted friends with expertise in youth development—some strategies for building youth ministry within the urban context. Our first step was seeking to fully understand the obstacles that confronted us as we sought to reach young people. I convened a group of local youth workers and youth pastors to discuss the challenges and difficulties we each faced at our particular posts. Some were in full- or part-time ministry, but most were dedicated lay people—such as basketball coaches, high school teachers, and pastors' wives with a passion for youth as well as firsthand experience in reaching and teaching them. We came up with a broad range of obstacles that were hindering us from reaching the teenagers around us. They are summarized below.

The Breakdown of the Urban Family

Today's urban churches are comprised of a conglomeration of battered, bruised, and broken people screaming out to Jesus to bring peace to their storm. They have families, but their traditional structures are as splintered and broken as are the people that make up the families. Consequently, their children do not fit the standard profile of youth to which most of us were trained to minister.

In all honesty, we don't know what to do with the half-children and stepchildren and grandchildren that are being raised between the pews. We don't know what to do with abused children, with those who have never seen their fathers, or those whose mothers are hooked on drugs or alcohol. We're unsure how to counsel their pain or answer their questions. Then we wonder why they refuse to attend our nice little youth services, and why they appear unmoved by our tidy messages.

We're ignorant to the fact that their lives are just not that neat. A messy message is needed for a messy people. A messy message is one that speaks of the mess created by real issues that have engulfed our modern-day lives. It's the kind of message that confronts child abuse and incest; that speaks to a lack of security, money, identity, and domestic peace.

I'm not saying that the inner city lacks strong families; it's just that most of them don't fit the traditional mold of what a family is "supposed" to look like. There are older sisters raising younger siblings because their momma had a breakdown; there are mothers doubling as fathers because of the disappearance of deadbeat dads. There are grandmothers who are raising their daughters' babies because their moms are incarcerated.

These families should not be castigated because they are not traditional, but celebrated because they have survived. Rather than being demonized, they should be enthusiastically supported because they are already on the verge of disintegration under the weight of poor options, poor choices, and poor chances.

Urban churches can no longer afford to shrink in the face of dysfunction, but instead must learn how to fully and boldly engage society with the unadulterated truth. The broken urban family is reaching out, but the arm of the church must be fully extended to reach it. We must structure holistic programs that reach the whole person and carry people when they cannot walk. Only as we begin to speak a real message to real people will we see real change in the fabric of our urban families.

The Graying of Church Leadership

Churches in our urban centers are dying—primarily because our leaders are dying. Innovation is dying, and our understanding of youth culture is dying. The great preachers of yesteryear are still preaching great messages, but they are preaching to congregations who are reflective of themselves in age, stature, and cultural background. So while our leadership is preaching good messages to good people, they miss the sinners as they preach to the choir.

The failure to train, teach, instruct, and then install the next generation of "pulpiteers" has placed our churches in jeopardy. Because the message has been correct but the methods have not been altered to fit the cultural context in which we now live, there is no effect. Moreover the church, facing a deep, dark vacuum of leadership, sacrifices the health and well-being of its own fathers by imploring them to hold on to the wheel of leadership long past their season of strength.

This tragedy cannot be blamed solely upon the church fathers. The sons of the church have been too impatient, scoffing at tradition and balking at protocol. Their lack of respect for the accomplishments of their elders has caused our fathers to withhold the pearls of their wisdom from the swine of youthful pride, and now we are all in trouble.

When a youth church (which we will describe later) embraces the message of yesteryear and shares it in a fresh way, community is powerfully impacted. When young ministers are trained and taught by seasoned church leaders, a continuity of thought, focus, and mission is achieved. It is essential for the "old lions" to raise young lions, or the pride will die.

The Death of Sunday School

Sunday school is dead. Nobody seems to want to go to Sunday school after age thirteen, and our inability to reach and teach teenagers in any other context is bringing about the death of our churches. Nevertheless, we cling like rats to the plank of a sunken ship as we hold on to our traditional Sunday school methods. Most of our denominational curriculum is based upon this Sunday school method, supplying antiquated methods that are true to the message but fail to reach their intended audiences. It's time to call the mourners, prepare the casket, buy the flowers, and dig a hole.

When youth ministry salvages the message of Sunday school and the structure of Sunday school, but is able to re-dress it in programs that speak relevantly to youth culture, young people will be impacted by the church. When the Christian education system within our churches more fully embraces young people, then youth culture will be changed by the gospel. And when teachers are given the liberty to reshape their curriculum to fit the needs of their students, then young people will be challenged to change.

The Lack of Effective, Full-Time Youth Pastors

Most churches in America are completely dependent upon the effectiveness of their Sunday school teachers and curriculum to raise young people into disciples. By contrast, I know of very few churches that depend solely upon those who teach their adult Sunday school classes to raise up their adult congregants.

It has been said that "a mist in the pulpit leaves a fog in the pew." Today's urban youth ministries are lost in the fog of mistrained, untrained, or poorly trained youth ministers who are rarely given the opportunity to preach or develop their gifting within the context of their local churches. In addition, the vast majority have never been mentored in the art and science of preaching. My heart has been broken to hear the homiletic weakness in America's youth pulpits.

The combination in many urban churches of a graying pulpit being replaced by an ineffective youth preaching staff is a recipe for continuing failure to raise up vibrant urban youth churches. And our churches' inability to train and teach young men and women how to preach the gospel effectively to their peers—and to provide ample opportunities for doing so—only promises to continue a cycle of defeat whereby the church fathers lose effective ministers to replace them, youth leaders lose the opportunity to sharpen their giftings, and the young people lose the opportunity to receive the Word with gladness.

The Absence of a Youth Movement

The last obstacle hindering the church from being viewed as vital and relevant to today's urban youth culture is its lack of momentum in creating a contemporary youth movement. One reason trendy youth fashions are so pervasive is that they are fresh, different, and mass-marketed to create a global impact and broad-based appeal to young people. Madison Avenue generates an active youth movement toward its seasonal collections; in doing so, it bombards the traditional modes and methods to carry its message.

Clothing designers and the stores that carry their products spend millions of dollars on television ads, radio spots, billboards, and magazines. They employ sports stars, rock stars, and movie stars to saturate the thinking, dreaming, and desires of young people to the point that they must have those "new" clothes. (It's interesting to note that most of the fashions being sold to today's youth as "new" are simply imitations of the fashions worn by youth of generations gone by. These old-fashioned fashions become trendy because the fashion outlets have mastered the control of the media outlets and thus have the ability to sell an old concept as a new commodity.)

The church must learn from Madison Avenue. We must begin to master the control of modern media outlets in order to affect a consistent message in the minds of today's youth. Churches should employ movie stars, rock stars, and athletic stars whose lives have been transformed by the life and work of Christ in order to make trendy the old message of the cross.

We must be able to utter "slick advertisement" and "the old rugged cross" in the same sentence if we are to generate and inseminate a Christian youth movement in the lives of today's youth. Local churches ought to purchase billboards, movie theaters, and sporting arenas. Radio spots and television spots should be utilized to reach young people within their local communities. Local churches should seek funding and support from local businesses in order to blanket the community with their purpose, presence, and products. We can no longer afford to keep the good news within the four walls of the church.

The Rise of the Urban Youth Church

After studying these factors and discussing them at length with my local ragtag team of youth workers, we began discussing some church-based solutions to address them. We began to imagine what a youth church—a church designed to reach and teach youth—might look like. From these imaginings, the first models for massive youth evangelistic services and lasting youth church designs were birthed in our area. I believe God began to inspire and show us that the message was still effective and the milieu was still effective; the weakness was in the methods our church was using to engage young people. We began to understand some distinct advantages to creating an urban youth church (UYC).

A Healthy Church Family

The UYC promotes the family. By standing in close covenant with the neighboring adult congregations, the UYC promotes a feeling of partnership and close family within the adult church community. By respectfully relating to its parent churches within the community, the youth church is not just another separate and free-standing church in the community. The urban community already has enough splintered church bodies. Rather, the UYC is related to the other churches in its community.

The UYC becomes a place where other parent bodies send and bring young people to find effective and contemporary youth ministry. Thus the urban youth church is not a stranger to the adult community of churches; it is their child. The urban youth church ministerial team receives counsel and support from the "elders" of its community even as it gives insight and training to church elders and other youth workers who are sent to serve in or around the UYC. Again, the UYC is part of the family. She constantly demonstrates the principles of mentorship on all levels, because her leadership is being actively mentored by the leaders of her parent churches.

This church family system or structure allows the youth church to strengthen the local churches within the community because, by design, it does not seek to duplicate their services but to diversify their ability to reach more young people with the gospel. A strong familial relationship between the youth church and the parental churches also allows young people to see a strong spiritual career path that can accommodate their growth as they age both biologically and spiritually.

So often, youth outreach ministries are unsuccessful at plugging new Christian young people into the fullness of the church. Thus, when the students who have been serviced by the youth ministry organization grow too old to be serviced by those youth programs, those youth are not prepared to merge into the mainstream church. But a UYC that constantly demonstrates a strong and close relationship with the local churches allows young people to see and understand the patterns and traditions of the adult congregations, making the transition into those churches as adults much more natural.

A Healthy Village

The urban youth church also promotes a strong family system by creating a place for young people to develop positive relationships with people who reside in healthy Christian homes. By making a way for people in the parent churches to serve as mentors and role models, the UYC can introduce kids from broken homes and nontraditional family systems to thriving, functional family systems. This may be their only opportunity to have close contact with healthy home systems.

As healthy adults serve as extended family members to broken young people, a Christian village is created within the local community. Church mothers become surrogate grandmothers to children who may never have had the privilege of building healthy cross-generational relationships. Deacon or trustee members from parental churches become community leaders who serve as healthy role models to the young people of the UYC. In essence, parental churches become adjunct staff for the UYC just through ongoing interaction of healthy role modeling and relationship building.

Thus, the UYC is not an independent, free-standing lone ranger in the urban community; it is the joint child of the other churches that inter-dependently serve the youth in a common community.

Bridging the Generational Leadership Gap

A healthy, functioning UYC provides a bridge between senior church leadership and up-and-coming youth leaders. Both groups of leaders are attempting to serve the people in the same community. The UYC creates a safer space for these two diverse and often divergent groups of leaders to both meet and talk. While younger urban leaders are often seeking mentors, fathers and mothers in the gospel desire to see how God would use them to pour into the next generation. As these connections are made, the gulf that has traditionally been present between youth ministry and adult ministry begins to narrow.

Relevant Teaching

The UYC does all the things that Sunday school was designed to do—that is, informing, instructing, and indoctrinating young people in the tenets of the faith. But it accomplishes these important tasks by using cutting-edge methods and modes of communication designed to reach, teach, and instruct today's urban young people. Dramas and skits, talk show formats, and PowerPoint presentations serve to better illustrate the glorious gospel of Jesus Christ to a media-savvy and high-tech-influenced generation.

Youth ministers' sermons, while they may be textual and expository in design, must also be topical and pragmatic in application if they are going to reach the hearts and souls of the youth in spiritual and practical ways. They must speak to the contemporary issues and challenges facing their young congregants and offer answers and hope to those who are often held in the dark and depressive grip of urban living today.

Besides expanding upon the Scriptures, youth ministers must also advocate for postsecondary education and training, speak on the efficacy of starting a business, or encourage buying a home. They must use the strength of the pul-pit to encourage young people to excel in their personal and professional lives, even as they are admonishing them to excel in their spiritual lives. The UYC must offer not only biblical training but life-skills training as well. It should teach the plan of salvation in the same setting that it teaches young people how to plan their budgets, balance their checkbooks, and get out of debt.

Interestingly, this is the way Sunday school used to function in society when it first started—teaching life skills, such as literacy, along with Bible truth.

The doctrines and dogmas of the church must be placed within the context of young peoples' practical needs if the power of God's Word is to be a foundational substructure for urban young people. Laying such a foundation is critical for the future development of strong and productive members of the parental churches within the community.

Creating a Youth Movement

Lastly, the urban youth church serves as a launching pad for large-scale evangelistic outreaches within the urban youth community. By sponsoring concerts and other large events, the UYC can reach out to those youth who attend as well as direct them to regular weekly services of parental churches in the area.

By unifying churches around reaching area youth, the UYC also contributes toward creating a momentum focused on changing the culture of urban teenagers. The UYC can help make religion cool in the minds of young people, and when the message becomes cool it spreads like fire throughout the region.

Adults will come and bring their young people to see the innovations and the creativity. Young people will bring themselves to the meetings. I have seen gang members try to bribe ushers to get them the best seats at such events. I have seen other young people steal cars so they could get to church on time. While I don't condone their methods, I appreciate their enthusiasm because it is such enthusiasm that helps to precipitate a youth movement.

Soon the T-shirts and fashion statements, the handshakes and catch phrases of the urban youth church begin to infiltrate the local youth culture. Instead of always having to build firewalls to keep the prevailing culture out of the church, the church begins to influence the prevailing culture. Gospel and Christian artists are heard at the clubs and suddenly the unchurched are interested in attending church outreach events so they can hear and see the crossover artists they have been hearing about from the youth congregates of the UYC.

Secular businesses suddenly are interested in sponsoring sports or artistic outreach teams, not so much because they totally agree with the leadership of the UYC but because they understand the advertisement opportunity that can be afforded them by being aligned with something so positive and popular in the youth community. Moreover, I have seen school systems and local city government become very open in their willingness to assist and partner with the UYC.

When done strategically in the power of the Holy Spirit, the UYC can become a uniting force for churches, local government, and businesses to reach thousands of young people with the glorious gospel and a practical message of hope and change that is so needed in our country's urban areas. Begin praying and bringing together key leaders in your community to see what God may have in mind for you.

Chapter 14
Developing Urban Student Leadership

Marvin A. Daniels

When people call my oldest son "Little Marvin," I pause and ponder whether that's good or bad. Have I transferred to him all that he needs in order to be equipped for all that God intends for his life? As he imitates me, will that lead him and others closer to Christ and his purposes?

Such is the essence of developing Christlike student leadership. Each generation has the responsibility of passing on the necessary character and quality traits to the next generation. If we criticize the generation following us, we must own the fact that they are merely reflecting what we have imparted to them. Our greatest charge is to reproduce a Christlike heritage in the children and youth who have been entrusted to us.

This is especially challenging given today's society and especially today's urban youth culture. Many of our youth are forming more relationships in chat rooms than with their next-door neighbors. As a result of our teaching them about inclusiveness, many have created their own customized religions. I've heard several teenagers in my area refer to themselves as Buddhist Catholics or Christian Muslims. Even among those who attend our churches, many are embracing other non-Christian forms of worship and rituals.

How will we regain our distinctive traits as biblical Christians? What will we leave this generation to pass on to the one that succeeds them? How can we help them know God intimately, obey Christ willingly, serve others lovingly, and impact society strategically? How do we insure that our youth groups become more than mere warehouses of activities, so that young people develop into spiritual leaders for God's kingdom? That's what this chapter is all about.

Leadership must be modeled, cultivated, and demonstrated. Therefore, to develop student leaders, I propose focusing on the following:

1. The power of presence

2. An appreciation for the process

3. A focus on the product

The Power of Presence

While walking through my neighborhood one day, I ran into one of the local drug dealers. Since I was fairly new to the community and I could see how successful he was in recruitment (he had children as young as six years old, as well as teenagers, picking up and delivering his product), I inquired about his strategy. He recognized me as the youth pastor from the corner church and greeted me politely. Then he said, "You know, Rev, when the kids leave their homes in the morning to go to school, they see me. And when they come home from school they see me. When they go to the store they see me. When they play in the park they see me. When they wait for the bus they see me. But when they want to see you, they got to go to your church."

His statement was very convicting. It also changed my strategy for reaching children and youth. He gave me a new understanding of the power of presence.

Simply being present does many things. First, it demonstrates to kids that we're interested in them. It shows them that they are important to us. It also gives them an opportunity to see what we are like, not just to hear what they're to be like. Developing student leadership demands our presence in their lives. There's no shortcut for it.

But presence must also be strategic, not haphazard. Drug dealers strategically select a location. They don't just show up anywhere. That could cost them their lives. Our presence must be strategic and intentional if we are to effectively develop student leaders.

When I go to visit Tyrone in his home, for example, it's not simply because I'm just in the neighborhood. I have been talking with him for months about the importance of respecting his parents and serving in his home. I want to see and hear if the lessons are being applied. And I've had Tyrone in my home as well so he can see how I live out these lessons of respect and servanthood.

When I tell young men how they should respect young ladies, I am modeling that in how I treat my wife. This gives credibility to my instruction so it's not just rhetoric. Student leadership always begins with adult leadership. It must first be modeled.

In a public school where I served as the mediation coordinator, it was my responsibility to help create a peaceable school climate where students had access to a mediation process to resolve their conflicts and disputes before potential harm occurred. To make this happen, I trained students to be peer-mediators who could assist their peers in utilizing this vehicle effectively.

Our number one task as mediators was to serve as examples inside and outside the school, with me being the lead example. I had to daily demonstrate in my own conflicts the example that I wanted my mediators to demonstrate before their peers. And then my mediators had to demonstrate those principles to their fellow students. If they were involved in fights in the hallways or on the streets, how could we expect others to conclude that mediation was an effective tool? Fortunately, they did buy into these principles and put them into practice. As a result, our school suspension rate decreased by 50 percent and the students came to view the school as a safe haven.

We in the church are notorious for teaching people biblical truths without living them out before them. Sometimes it's simply that we teach from a distance—as that local drug dealer accused me of doing. Other times, our actions negate our words. Authentic presence understands that

· we are the mirrors into which young people look,

· we can't take kids further than we ourselves have gone, and

· faith can be caught and transferred.

Two years after my first encounter with our neighborhood drug dealer, he dropped into one of our evening programs where some of his would-be recruits were gathered. I walked over to him and said softly, "I took your advice." He shook his head, obviously recalling our earlier conversation, and then walked out. Thanks to his stinging comment years earlier, I am all the more committed to making sure my neighborhood youth see me and others from the Christian community as they board the bus, play in the park, go to the store—and now, praise God—enter our churches. That's the power of presence.

An Appreciation for the Process

When developing a student leadership team, you must distinguish between a project and a process. A project is a temporary, organized effort that creates a unique deliverable product, service, or plan. A process continues on with no defined end. Student leadership is a process.

Luke 2:52 illustrates a wonderful developmental model of holistic growth. It says, "And Jesus grew in wisdom and stature, and in favor with God and men." The key word is *grew*. There was a process taking place in his maturation. Likewise, we must allow our students to experience the process of growth into leadership and not be focused merely on the ultimate outcome.

Our teenagers need to know what it is like to struggle and prepare for an activity, wrestle with the responsibility of evangelism, try to display servant-hood in their homes, know the lonely feeling of leaving the crowd instead of following it, and experience the trials of living righteously. Here are a few thoughts on how to take students through such a process:

· Have a clear understanding of discipleship. It's life-on-life, not classroom sessions talking about life.

· Leave room for failure while still maintaining biblical standards.

· Don't tell youth they can be anything they want to be; that implies that they already possess all the gifts and talents that exist. Instead, help them discover their individual gifts and talents.

· Don't applaud mediocrity. Push students to fulfill their commitments.

· Hold students accountable. Their business (the way they live) is your business, and your business (the way you live) is theirs.

· Realize that you and your students are on a journey that's continuous.

Part of this process involves engaging others beyond our young people's immediate peer context. A few years ago I facilitated a meeting between our youth and the senior adults in our church. Each group interviewed the other about their past and present lives. As the youth heard stories about the successes and failures of their elders, whom they had assumed were outdated and irrelevant members of society, they gained a new appreciation for just how much wisdom and understanding they possessed.

Likewise, our "senior saints," who otherwise viewed our teenagers as loud, rebellious, and disrespectful, began to empathize with the issues they were struggling with. As a result of that event, our student leadership team decided to include some of these elder brothers and sisters on their advisory council.

Another vital element in the process of developing student leadership involves the training and equipping of our students. There is no sport I know of where the coach is satisfied with simply giving players information without requiring some form of practical application. No football coach is interested in how well you can read the playbook; he wants to know if you understand it and can execute it effectively. That's why football players practice! Yet oftentimes we give our kids lots of information from the playbook (the Bible) and assume we've done our job. We seldom practice with them.

The problem is that we in the church have operated from a paradigm of institutionalized faith for a long time. We have assumed that faith is primarily nurtured in local church buildings. But if we hope to effectively pass on our faith, we must be willing to make a radical shift in our understanding of the process of cultivating leadership. We must connect young people's faith to their families, churches, communities, and culture; and then provide them with opportunities to practice living out that faith in each of those contexts.

A Focus on the Product

The products of our ministries are our children and youth. The Apostle Paul referred to those in the church he founded at Philippi as "my joy and crown" (Philippians 4:1). While we can't take responsibility for their growth and the decisions they alone can make, we need to remember that they are the focus of our ministry. It's not the big programs we may create but how young lives are transformed that matters.

As we invest our time, energy, skills, and lives into the development of our youth, God graciously allows us to see some of the fruit of those labors. They may not all turn out as we hope, but if we stay at it long enough we do get the privilege of seeing fruit.

I remember a young man who was extremely impressionable when I first met him. He had many influences upon his life, but one night after a week-long church event he came up to me and said, "I've been listening to you for a long time, but I've also been watching you. And if Jesus is like you, I want to get to know him."

I was quick to tell him that Jesus was not like me. If he hung around me long enough, he would see my flaws and discover that I would let him down. But I also told him that I am who I am because of Jesus, and thanked him for the compliment. What he was really saying was that my words and my life matched up, and that was something he was looking for. It reminded me of the awesome responsibility we have as youth workers to live authentic, Holy

Spirit-filled lives before those we are called to minister to.

That boy is a young man now. He is a youth outreach worker for a public school system. His influence upon young males in both elementary and high school is phenomenal. He has received citations from the mayor's office for his impact upon these young at-risk males. Many have re-enrolled in school and now attend his weekly Bible studies, too. I praise God that he used me in this young man's life, and that somehow I have a share in the joy and crown of all the young people he is touching!

Truly, there's no better place to invest than in the leadership development of today's urban teenagers. As ambassadors to our cities, we have the privilege and responsibility to "tell the next generation the praiseworthy deeds of the Lord, his power, and the wonders he has done...so the next generation would know them, even the children yet to be born, and they in turn would tell their children" (Psalm 78:4, 6).

Chapter 15
Developing Mission-Driven Programs

Chris Troy

nthony, who lives in one of the toughest housing projects in Boston, tells me in the context of playing pool together: "Nobody in this neighborhood here ever changes. It's just not possible."

Having visited Anthony's home, I can understand his line of thinking. Every time I go there, the shades are drawn and the rooms are dark, with only the television on. People are watching TV at all hours of the day and night. Anthony exhibits no positive outlook for his future whatsoever.

Similarly, as I drive Lupo home, I ask him why he doesn't go to school. He replies matter-of-factly that he's been kicked out of two schools, he isn't in his right grade, and he is currently on probation—so why should he even try when nobody really wants him there? He isn't even mad or sad when he says this; he's just giving an honest assessment of his situation. He adds, "Who is really going to care one way or another, anyway?"

Developing a Programmatic Strategy

My experiences with young people like Anthony and Lupo have greatly shaped my ministry. I have grown in my understanding of how to develop a ministry that really helps kids experience the abundant life of Christ here and now. This understanding has grown out of a process of bringing Scripture to the life issues of young people and then bringing those life issues and questions back to Scripture, so as to form an unending circle—I call this the hermeneutical circle. Effectively doing so insures that our message doesn't become stale or disconnected with life and that it speaks relevantly to those we are called to serve.

Program development done in this way also helps keep our ministry activities rooted in Scripture while still addressing the issues, struggles, and concerns of our young people. It further helps us prevent one of the greatest mistakes ministries often make—undertaking a program simply because someone else did it or because there is an apparent need. Developing programs in this way often leads to futility, as there usually is no underlying mission to guide and regularly assess our individual programs.

Defining a Mission Statement and Methodology

For a ministry to develop a comprehensive and effective approach that helps young people experience the abundant life of Christ, without becoming fragmented or overwhelmed by the weight of its programs, it needs the glue of a mission statement. Using the process of the hermeneutical circle, which I referred to earlier, can help us develop a mission statement that in turn can help us channel the energies of our organization into a focused effort so it does not become disjointed.

An effective mission statement focuses on what the institution is really trying to accomplish, and then allows everybody in the organization to say to themselves, "This is how I help reach the goal."

A mission statement is different from having vision. I've found that most urban youth ministry professionals have no lack of vision or commitment, yet they are often frustrated by their lack of impact. This, I believe, is rooted in a lack of training, resources, and a mission-driven strategy for ministry. Mission statements are crucial for us to develop the right programs, determine the level of our effectiveness, and gather the appropriate resources to fulfill a mission. They also guide us in equipping our staff and volunteers for ministry.

One example of a clear and descriptive mission statement comes from the Girl Scouts. The statement reads, "In partnership with committed adult volunteers, girls develop leadership skills, strong values, and social conscience that will serve them all their lives."[1] As you read this, you can immediately envision the types of programs you would need to develop to accomplish such a mission. Their mission statement grew out of their experience and understanding of girls today, and the unique role they could play in addressing those issues.

Alongside the need for a clear mission statement is a concise ministry methodology. Our Boston Urban Youth Foundation's ministry methodology involves the following:

- Sharing the love of Christ in word and deed
- Building strong mentoring relationships with young people
- Exposing young people to the abundant opportunities available to them
- Motivating and inspiring young people to be and do their very best
- Assisting youth in focusing on activities that will insure their success
- Facilitating the development of the necessary skills to fulfill their potential

Both our mission statement and our ministry methodology are summarized in our ministry brochure, which says: "The Boston Urban Youth Foundation was incorporated in 1992 with a mission 'to help young people develop spiritually, emotionally, academically, and economically.' BUYF combines creative programs with committed adults who spend time with young people to instill hope, vision, and a positive future in their lives."

Our mission statement combined with our ministry methodology is what guides BUYF in all of its program activities. If a program doesn't contribute to fulfilling our mission and isn't consistent with our stated methodology, it's not a program we should be doing.

Developing a Strategy

Determining what strategies to take is what tests both our leadership and the strength of our ministry. It's hard work, and most effective when undertaken as a team.

I find some invaluable lessons in a couple of stories contained in the Gospel of Mark. First is the story of the paralytic brought before Christ in Mark 2:1-12. His friends had a clear mission. They wanted to bring their paralyzed friend before Jesus. Pulling it off would require a team of people. They worked together to overcome the obstacle of an overcrowded house. They planned, improvised, and executed the act of bringing their friend before Christ, even though it meant creatively lowering him through the roof! It takes a team to bring someone to the feet of Christ.

In Mark 9:14-29, the disciples could not help the father of a son who was demon possessed. Perplexed, they finally came to Jesus. His response was that they needed to pray. Persistent prayer, fasting, and faith can change the impossible. While I'm not perfect in the spiritual discipline of prayer, I have been much more prayerful in recent years because of my desire to see our young people experience the abundant life of Christ. I have come to realize that no matter how creative our programs are, the battles are won and lost in the spiritual realm. If you have any doubt about that, consider Hector.

Hector is a fifteen-year-old drug dealer who often comes into our center to check us out. We see him every Friday night, but he will not come in any farther than the doorway. Hector has experienced every type of abuse you can imagine and is very streetwise. Over the course of his fifteen years, he has lived on the streets, used drugs and alcohol to excess, committed his life to Christ, been in a car accident that put him in a wheelchair until rods could be inserted into his legs, attempted suicide, been to prison twice, and nearly been deported.

He still wrestles with God, but in the midst of all this he has found peace with himself and God. Through every ordeal he has faced, the followers of Christ who have stuck with him in constant prayer and encouragement have made the difference. Our strategy must include prayer.

Designing a Program

Once you're clear about your mission, methodology, and strategy, designing programs comes much more naturally. Ideas begin to flow freely, each generating tremendous excitement. Unfortunately, most great ideas never get out of the idea stage.

In each of the ministry programs I have played a role in launching, we've followed a process that has helped to insure that the program actually got off the ground and could be sustained. This process involved bringing together a group of people who were willing to meet weekly or monthly to help bring an idea to reality. I made sure this group had expertise beyond my own, to think through those issues that I may not have been remotely aware of. In each case these groups have also provided me with the necessary accountability to keep the project moving. There's nothing more motivating than having to prepare for a meeting with people who are there voluntarily! Although not every idea has worked out as I thought, we were able to get all the projects launched and running for a minimum of three years.

Let me share a couple of examples of how this process has worked for us. The first is our economic development program.

The Youth Enterprise Project

The birth of the Youth Enterprise Project was deeply rooted in our mission statement and the issues we saw confronting our young people. In the late

1980s and early '90s, drugs and violence were ripping apart our city. Many of the young men involved with our program had little hope of breaking out of the cycle of poverty they lived in and didn't see how they could follow Christ when about the only available means to making money was the illegal marketplace of the streets.

Our ministry already had vigorous values clarification programs: evangelization, camps, mentoring, and Bible studies. Yet we were having a tough time competing with the street economy. Believing that our young people were extremely gifted, but clueless as to how those gifts could be used in our nation's economic system, I gathered together a group of business people I knew to ask for their guidance in launching an economic development ministry. Each of these people was incredibly gifted—many had M.B.A.'s from Harvard or MIT. Each also possessed a knowledge of business I couldn't come close to, while I had an understanding of urban youth ministry that they lacked.

We met monthly at 6:30 a.m. for a year, since this was the best time for them to meet. We researched other programs, met with kids to do market research, and began to develop what we now call the Youth Enterprise Project. The program has consistently sought to help young people identify their marketable gifts and abilities so they might become more motivated and focused on doing what's required for a positive future. While our focus has been on creating small businesses for youth to run, we have also helped other young people get meaningful jobs in the business community.

Of course it hasn't all been a smashing success. One time one of our guys was caught sleeping at the computer. Another faked his phone calls and told his supervisor that he had just spoken to someone who the supervisor later learned was deceased.

But then there are other stories, like Michael's. He was being courted by the gangs when I met him. I helped him get a job interview at a law firm. When he met with the attorney, the attorney told Michael that this wasn't like *L.A. Law*, and that he wasn't even sure what he could pay him.

On the way home Michael said, "Chris, I'll take anything. I'm just a kid from Roxbury." So Michael started at the law firm. At the end of the summer I took him out for dinner and he reported that he wasn't interested in the gang stuff anymore. Today Michael has his M.A. in education and is a teacher in the Boston public school system. Hope and vision can take a kid a long way!

School Success Truancy Program

The second example is our School Success Truancy Program. It came about as a result of a meeting that was designed to help initiate a first-time offender program. With several leaders from law enforcement and the church, we were discussing a first-time offender program. I asked if there was an earlier time to intervene than when a kid gets arrested. The district attorney responded, "Yes—truancy."

He went on to say that over 50 percent of all inmates were truants. From that point forward we focused on truancy. For a year, a group of us met monthly to develop a truancy intervention program. Our research uncovered the fact that Boston had only eight truancy officers and 6,000 truants. We also learned that 34 percent of all students in the Boston school system were truants, and that there were no privately run truancy programs in our city.

After a year of planning, we launched our School Success Truancy Program, which today serves 250 middle-school truants. We had some problems the first year when we tried to be in nine schools. Having learned from our mistakes, we scaled down the initiative to three schools so we could build stronger partnerships with fewer schools. As a result, we were able to double the number of youth we served from year one to year two.

With a program objective of improving both school attendance and performance, School Success fits well with our organization's mission and methodology. It also gave us a more defined target population on which to focus. Starting School Success has forced us to look at improving the rest of our ministry when it comes to helping our young people academically. As a result, we launched our Academic Enrichment Center to focus on improving school performance in all of our youth.

A synergistic energy happens when complementary programs are united under a common mission. For example, a year after our School Success program was launched, we knew we were doing a good job of holding young people accountable, but many of them still lacked the motivation to do well in school. For years we had been running successful college tours for kids in our weekly club, but now it made sense to develop similar college tours exclusively for truant students. It worked. These students' attitudes and conversation changed dramatically when they began to be motivated by long-term vision.

Johnny was one of the students who went on our college tour. He was a bit of a pain, but we all knew he had a lot of potential. Even though he locked everyone out of the van at a rest stop because he couldn't have the front seat, he set his sights on Howard University. His high school grades went from D's and F's to A's and B's. Johnny graduated in the spring of 2002 with a B.A. in business, thanks to a vision God placed in his heart during a college tour.

Measuring Outcomes

Measuring programmatic outcomes is a critical discipline often over-looked by ministries. Yet if we are to be good stewards of our resources, we must be willing to look objectively at the impact our programs have on the youth we serve.

When I say measuring outcomes, I don't mean keeping track of how many kids showed up for Bible study. While it's important that kids show up, it's more important to know that their showing up is making a difference in their lives. From a fundraising perspective, showing outcomes is going to be increasingly more important as donors consider where to best invest their resources. The promise of services alone will no longer attract major resources.

Measuring outcomes requires us to clarify our ministry objectives as well as to think through how we will measure the outcomes of our ministry. While grades, attendance, and going on to college are very objective measurements, how do we measure spiritual development? One way we have accomplished this is through questionnaires.

Through the use of questionnaires, we have also discovered that service projects have been one of our most powerful tools for evangelizing and discipling our youth. While suburban youth are often given opportunities to participate in missions trips, urban teenagers are seldom given the blessing of serving others, and receiving the blessing in return.

When we brought our young people to Mexico City, they returned far more grateful for the blessings in their lives. They also learned how much of a blessing serving others can be, and began to gain an awareness of their responsibility to those around them who are less fortunate. The overall impact on the spiritual lives of our young people has been astounding.

One Kid at a Time

I began this chapter with stories of some of the angst and issues many of our young people struggle with. Their issues, combined with Scripture, have shaped the mission of the Boston Urban Youth Foundation. Our staff and board have participated in the development of a programmatic strategy that seeks to fulfill our stated mission of helping young people experience the abundant life of Christ. Out of a sense of stewardship with our resources, we have begun to measure outcomes to better determine the effectiveness of our programs and make the necessary changes to improve our efforts.

But in closing I want to emphasize the relational nature of this kind of ministry (hence our slogan: "One Kid at a Time"). This type of work is a process. Change happens, but not always on our timeline. Yet I have found that the elements we've focused on in this chapter keep us hanging in there, walking alongside our young people, so that we will "not become weary in doing good, for at the proper time we will reap a harvest if we do not give up" (Galatians 6:9).

Endnote

[1] Girl Scouts Web site, http://www.girlscouts.org

Chapter 16
Developing Holistic Ministry Programs Through Creative Use of Resources
Karin M. Wall, LICSW

n the mid- to late 1980s, a number of changes took place on the urban landscape. Neighborhood gentrification created a housing shortage as well as huge rent increases; school systems were producing marginal graduates; unemployment was on the rise, as was the rate of teenage pregnancy; and crack cocaine use exploded. Urban centers were erupting with violence—and Boston, Massachusetts, was no exception.

It was against this backdrop that Bruce Wall Ministries, Inc. (BWM), was founded. Using a passionate youth pastor with a unique position and standing in the community, and me—his social worker wife—God breathed into being a concept of comprehensive youth ministry focused on promoting the healthy growth and development of youth and families spiritually, socially, economically, and educationally. Through telling the story of how BWM came into being, I hope to provide practical insights and transferable models that you can use as you develop holistic ministry tailored around your own community's needs. I will also pay specific attention to the ways BWM found and leveraged resources for these programs at each stage of development.

Background

Like many urban youth workers, my husband Bruce Wall served two decades in dual vocations as court magistrate of the Boston Juvenile Court and as the youth minister at a church in Boston. Because of his unique perspective, he caught early sight of the rapidly changing characteristics of youth culture in general, and the urban brand in particular. He foresaw that for the twenty-first-century church to be relevant, effective, and authentic, it would have to radically change the way it "did church," especially youth ministry. No longer could a wayward teenager be told, "I know you were taught better than that" or "I know you learned better than that in church." For most, church was a foreign place.

As a result, Bruce was commissioned by his church to "set up shop" at a skating rink located in the heart of the city that attracted upwards of 200 youth on weekends. I wanted no part of this venture. I was a clinical social worker with a passion for African-American history, and that was that. But God inserted himself into my plans shortly after our first child was born. He issued me a challenge to "do for other children what I would want done for my own, should I be unable to provide for them."

We adopted 1 Corinthians 12:12-26 as our guiding Scripture. "The body is a unit, though it is made up of many parts; and though all its parts are many, they form one body. So it is with Christ" (I Corinthians 12:12). Chiseling this passage into our spirits and wrestling with its implications began to give definition and dimension to our work. It became an anchor for the staff and board, and drew like-minded individuals and organizations into partnership with us.

BWM's initiatives have evolved largely in response to community needs. The clear definition of our mission came from first being open to seeing what the needs were and then being open to responding to them. Although we had a general sense of what the youth in our community needed based on our experiences, we allowed ourselves to be teachable and responsive to what we heard from God, the kids, and their families. We also paid attention to the research that was beginning to come out on urban violence from law enforcement and the social work community.

Then we began to step out in faith for God's vision for BWM, not our own limited human vision and perspective. All BWM initiatives and undertakings are weighed against God's calling, timing, and opportunity. Ministries or programs that meet needs are necessary and biblical, but they in themselves do not cause people to change. The only lasting change comes from an encounter with Jesus the Holy One, followed by nurturing and discipling in a local assembly.

We can have the best-laid plans of men and the best means of executing them, and even the necessary resources, but it is God who produces the fruit. This passage also teaches us that we have a role to play in the same way that the person being ministered to does.

The Early Years

The first five years of this ministry were spent primarily learning and forming our identity. Part of that learning involved assessing the needs of our community. As a result of that, it made sense that the neighborhood roller skating rink was the best vehicle through which to establish a ministry to reach the unchurched youth of our area.

The Chez Vous skating rink had been in the community for decades, and it carried a good reputation even among those in their fifties who remembered frequenting it as teenagers themselves. But now it was filled every night with hip-hop teenagers.

We got permission from the owner of the rink to begin having a "Gospel Night," where only contemporary gospel music was played while kids skated. The youth who had been coming and listening to hip-hop were not going to let a little gospel music stop them, and so the number of skaters stayed constant. Our handful of staff were there to skate, interact, and give a thinly veiled sermon at the end of the evening. Soon we were hosting rallies, gang truces, and concerts there.

Before long, however, our very strength—attracting large numbers of youth—became our vulnerability. With such large numbers of relatively unsupervised youth, in combination with the new turf wars of that time, Chez Vous had been written off by many as a problem spot. Fights between warring gang factions after closing were routine. City buses often refused to pick up teenagers at that stop for fear of trouble on their buses.

Bruce negotiated a plan with the city police, transportation police, and transportation department whereby assigned buses were dispatched to pick up kids as Chez Vous let out, with the support of police at the stops and on the buses. This proved to be very effective in the long run. Residents felt safe, and the police became part of the solution rather than waiting for the usual Friday or Saturday night calls to respond to mini-riots at Chez Vous.

Before long, sports figures, Christian rap artists, police, and local politicians were coming to Chez Vous to host other events to support the community. We began hanging out there after school too, as we began to respond to the requests of young people who were asking for a safe place to be after school. It was through the time spent tutoring young people on their homework that we began to hear their stories about school, home, older siblings, parents, and so on.

Although BWM was new on the scene with a scant track record and very little money, we began to identify and use the resources we did have to build more. That's where our dual professions came in handy. For instance, while a parent or sibling was not likely to pay attention to a "minister" urging their attendance at a meeting, or welcome a home visit from a "pastor's wife," they would respond to the intervention, referral, or recommendation of a social worker and/or court official they were likely to see—or had seen—in juvenile court!

We soon found ourselves doing intervention work at home, in court, and at school; involved in mediation between rival gangs; and advocating on behalf of kids for jobs, housing, and other services.

Lessons Learned From Our Early Experiences

- Learn to listen well. Be confident in what you know, but know there is more to learn.

- Take inventory. You probably have more resources than you think.

- Take time to reach agreement on your mission. It will anchor you.

- Don't take yourself too seriously. God is the one making a difference in the lives of people.

- Don't cut corners on good financial management.

- Collaboration is great, but take the time to build a relationship with your collaborator; otherwise, it's merely a business arrangement.

- Nurture a culture within your organization.

- Make prayer a central core value.

- Recognize that there is reciprocity in ministry. You will give as well as receive.

- Know when it's time to go.

The Transitional Years

After we had been established nearly five years, the needs of the ministry exceeded what could be offered at the roller rink. Bruce had just stepped down from his court magistrate position and I, too, was fully employed by BWM. Shortly after, Bruce was asked to pastor a church just three miles from the rink, and we saw that as a way to merge together the mission of BWM with a church that could be focused on enfolding these new young Christians. Today many of the initiatives we provide to the community under BWM are housed at the church, but they remain under the separate domain of Bruce Wall Ministries, Inc.

Following are descriptions of some of the programs we developed in these transitional years.

Camp Ozioma (Good News) was launched as a Christian summer day camp infused with African-American history and academics. Using the seven principles of Kwanzaa—unity, self-determination, purpose, faith, cooperative economics, collective work and responsibility, and creativity—as the basis for each week's camp theme, all Scripture and activities matched that week's principle. Camp is what we call our "full court press," because it gives us the greatest exposure to kids over a consistent and concentrated length of time.

Project 21 (P21) is the successor to the basic tutorial efforts started at the skating rink. Its name serves as a reminder of our responsibility to shepherd young people to their twenty-first birthdays and into the twenty-first century. This program idea came as the result of hearing more and more young boys say they had no vision for the future because they literally could not see themselves living to see their twenty-first birthdays! This type of thinking is one of the tragic byproducts of living with increasing levels of community violence, death, hopelessness, despair, and marginalization. P21 focuses on academics as a vehicle for achievement—one that allows young people to see themselves as successful investors in the future.

PREP (Partnering Resources to Enable Productivity) was launched in response to the changes brought about by welfare reform legislation in 1997, which placed time limits on the receipt of welfare benefits. Suddenly we were faced with the need to examine what, if anything, we could do, should do, or were being called to do in response to this change in policy. We began to offer instructor-led courses on a semester basis in a state-of-the-art computer technology center. Our computer lab is open to the public daily, providing free computer and Internet access.

The goal of PREP is to minister to the practical needs of many in our community who are in need of skills that will enable them to enter the job market, upgrade their skills, or break the feeling of isolation that plagues many of our senior citizens. It underscores the 1 Corinthians 12 principle by partnering with two other churches as well as the Boston police, who offer a computer skills training program to newly released inmates.

New Horizons was birthed from a sobering conversation with a thirteen-year-old boy who had been at camp and in our after-school program for five years. One day he declared to us that his intentions for the following summer were to follow in the footsteps of older cousins and siblings and sell drugs, since he would be too old for camp. We realized that youth uninvolved in sports, part-time employment, or other extracurricular activities were somehow expected to responsibly supervise themselves, placing them at very high risk for criminal activity—often out of sheer boredom.

The objective of New Horizons is to match adolescents with meaningful adult mentors who model a positive lifestyle, strong faith, and a meaningful profession. We aim to help kids think through the important issues of adolescence and direct them toward the next phase of their lives beyond high school graduation.

Resource Development

Resource development is becoming more and more difficult to do. This is partly because churches and parachurch organizations are growing rapidly in the city, and with such growth comes a much greater need for finances.

Churches no longer question whether it is appropriate for them to sponsor after-school programs, summer camps, food banks, job development programs, counseling services, housing programs, and recovery programs. Such faith-based organizations are no longer a novelty in most major cities.

That's the good news. The bad news is that with all the nonprofit organizations in the United States, most of them operate on very small annual budgets, which means lots of programs with worthwhile goals and objectives are looking for supplemental funding to keep themselves afloat. Simply put, there is a lot more competition today for the same amount of giving dollars.

As a result, when it comes to acquiring and managing resources, nonprofit organizations in the twenty-first century must be more strategic and efficient than ever before if they hope to survive. Fortunately, there is a lot of good material, training, and technical assistance available to help in these areas. It takes more than a heart for reaching kids to manage a thriving ministry these days. Based on your ministry's needs and capabilities, familiarize yourself with the best sources for resource development. Below are some brief suggestions.

Fees

Each of the programs we offer adults in the community charges a modest fee to its recipients. While they are all not-for-profit programs and don't generate a lot of revenue, requiring fees serves several purposes:

• Requiring fees takes some of the financial pressure off a ministry's overall budget.

• When a parent pays for camp, or when a student pays even a modest fee for a computer course, there is a sense of buy-in that encourages a fuller partnership, as opposed to the feeling of being a passive recipient of services.

• Paying a fee for service gives each person a universal language that can be taken into the marketplace to friends, neighbors, and colleagues—people usually ask, "How much did it cost you?"

Individuals

Individuals can be your most stable and viable sources of resources. Not only will individuals give of their finances; they will often volunteer, tell others about your organization, and make in-kind donations. Individuals will be faithful, but they require development and maintenance.

One example comes to mind of an elderly couple who had known Bruce since he was a teenager. They had been lifelong residents of Boston and saw our work as something close to their hearts and as an important and valuable asset to the community. They relished receiving our newsletter, loved getting occasional thank you notes from us for various things, and from time to time showed up at events. They also wrote a monthly check to the ministry for more than ten years straight—never once skipping a month. I believe their faithfulness to BWM was the result of our keeping in touch with them enough that they felt connected to us.

Other Churches

Another common and traditional form of support comes from the missions budgets of other churches that are in partnership with you. This is a great example of the "one body, many parts" principle. Churches from other parts of the same city, or the suburbs, who may not have a desire or calling to serve the city firsthand can get involved through supporting you. To cultivate this requires high-engagement relationships with churches so that they truly feel they are in partnership and not just a funding source.

Having such relationships can lead to other means of involvement such as volunteers, prayer support, assistance with fundraising, technical assistance, and joint projects. For example, we've undertaken many joint projects with other churches we have had longstanding relationships with, such as a 1994 joint missions trip to Tennessee to assist in the rebuilding of five black churches that had been burned down due to arson attacks.

Foundations

Foundations tend to be the funding source that everyone gravitates toward. They require initial prospecting to determine compatibility with your mission, interests, and programs.

Most states have an Associated Grant Makers library that provides a resource manual with foundation listings. These provide an excellent profile of every foundation, its priorities, the procedure for applying to them, the contact person, how much they give away each year in grants, what their average grant size is, and proposal deadlines. There is usually a common proposal form that even an inexperienced proposal writer can respond to.

There are also lots of workshops on grant writing that are offered free of charge or for a small fee. Hiring grant writers can be expensive, but it is sometimes possible to job-share such a position with another organization and split the cost of the position. Another option is to hire a freelance grant writer to develop your proposal for a flat fee and give you a list of appropriate foundations who may be interested.

If you have relationships with other nonprofit organizations or churches, ask to see one of their successful proposals, not for the purpose of plagiarizing, but to get a sense of what a well-written proposal looks like.

Once you get your foot in the door with a foundation, depending on the culture of the foundation, you may gain an advocate for your organization. You can then take advantage of trainings they may offer their grantees. Some foundations may require your participation. Look at this training as a blessing, not a threat or imposition. For example, BWM's affiliation as a grantee of the Faith in Action Committee of the United Way of Massachusetts Bay requires that BWM learn an outcomes measurement method. This has only served to strengthen our efforts and increase our capacity as an organization.

Corporations

Corporate sponsors tend to be multiyear sponsors. Corporations also have priorities just like foundations and any other funding source. While some philanthropists will want to remain anonymous, most corporations will welcome publicity. Often corporations who may be interested support events and make various in-kind donations.

There was a time when we were trying to turn a small lot adjacent to the church into a playground. We worked with a corporate sponsor. In one day, their volunteers and ours painted, landscaped, and erected all the structures. At the end of the day the mayor and several local sports figures dedicated the area.

Local, State, and Federal Government

The application process tends to be the most tedious and labor intensive for this type of funding. The cost of assigning staff, particularly for a small organization, to respond to the many requests of the government must be weighed against the benefit of receiving the grant. There also tends to be little assistance in navigating through the application process, aside from initial bidders' conferences, which are sometimes mandatory.

Increasingly government RFPs (requests for proposals) tend to require some type of partnership between community, city, and other agencies such as schools. Partnerships or collaborations can be a great way to get your feet wet and introduced to the funding world. Securing a few successful partnerships can help you build momentum and continue to grow.

We have partnered with the Boston Police on several violence prevention initiatives. They needed community partners; we needed the resources and were already providing the service. Connecting with them allowed us to upgrade our capacity.

At the end of a successful partnership, the door is always open for future ventures, your ministry's visibility has increased through your relationship with a known entity, and you have built mutually satisfying relationships.

By definition, God's people should be part of the solution to the ills of the culture and society we live in. Good ideas that are God-inspired and turn into ministry are propelled by a drive toward excellence that draws people to God's good works. It's exciting work!

Chapter 17
The Power of Partnerships Between Urban and Suburban Youth Ministries

Rev. Alvin C. Bibbs Sr.

Over the past twenty years, I have observed the formation of partnerships from many different perspectives. For several years I served as head basketball coach at a Chicago public high school, observing students as they struggled to lay down their individual interests for the sake of the team. Later I served as a university assistant basketball coach, again observing young adults wrestle through how they could make a name for themselves at the university and beyond. My journey continued to the world of Major League baseball and the National Football League, as I examined how difficult it was for adult men to trust each other long enough to understand the value of teamwork.

Outside the world of sports, I have had numerous partnership experiences as a youth minister. In my position as a regional director with Young Life ministries, God used me to play a role in connecting mainline local churches in under-resourced urban and rural communities with predominately white-led parachurch organizations. Seeing brothers and sisters from such diverse backgrounds come together to reach young people with the saving message of Jesus Christ was something only God could orchestrate!

For the past several years I have been the director of extension ministries at Willow Creek Community Church in Chicago. The common thread to all these experiences is that I can bear witness to the power of intentional and proactive teamwork and partnerships.

It has been stated that when a team is working at its best you can point to "team chemistry." That happens when everyone knows what the game plan is, knows what it will take to accomplish the task, and has an undying commitment to do their part. The same is true for urban youth ministry partnerships. This chapter focuses on the processes that must be in place in order to effectively navigate ministry and develop a chemistry that amplifies God's voice in the city. These partnership lessons are absolutely essential for your ministry's success in our ever changing and complex society.

The Essence of Partnership— A Biblical Model

Mark 2:1-12 is one of my favorite passages of Scripture. It describes beautifully the nature of strategic ministry partnerships. In it Mark shares the account of friends being called into action with each other to assist their paralyzed friend.

What I love about this picture of true partnership are the many transferable lessons we can learn through this story.

Have Faith

First, these guys were so determined to get their friend to the feet of Jesus that no obstacle could stand in their way. It was their *faith* and *belief* that Jesus could heal their friend that called them into action, and it was their faith that called Jesus into action to assist their friend. At its core, that's what partnership is all about: *a call to action.*

I remember Easter Sunday 1975 like it was yesterday. I headed to the theater with my friends after church to check out the latest movie in downtown Chicago. As we were walking down the sidewalk to the nearest bus stop, I suddenly disappeared from sight! Not paying attention to where I was walking, I had fallen into an open sewer. After realizing what had happened, my friends quickly ran to my aid and devised a plan to get me out of there. Because I had hurt my leg, they had to carry me home horizontally. My parents then rushed me to the nearest hospital to make sure everything was okay.

That experience has served to help me relate, at least a little bit, to the man in Mark 2. I would have been in big trouble without the assistance of my five high school buddies. I never could have gotten out of that hole, let alone gotten home, without their assistance. What an awesome display of comfort, friendship, love, and teamwork by my peers, as they worked to get me home safely. God was answering my desperate prayers as I lay helplessly in the arms of friends who were carrying me home. The same principle is true in ministry partnerships: When potential ministry partners are of one mind, purpose, and spirit, Jesus will also respond to our prayers.

Create a Vision

The faith of each member of this unique partnering team that Mark described held a compelling and inspiring vision. Through their collective vision, they could visualize their friend talking and walking among them. They knew it was possible if they believed in Jesus' miraculous power and in each other.

In partnership, it is imperative that some inspired leader articulates a compelling vision to inspire others to act according to the charge given. Undoubtedly one of these men had a vision of how to get their friend to the feet of Jesus so he could be healed. At some point he must have shared that vision with the rest of the group, and the energy among them must have become contagious. Otherwise, they never would have been able to pull off what they did. For what they were attempting to accomplish certainly was not average or typical. A clear vision allows a leader to take people or an organization to places they have never experienced before.

Formulate a Strategy

Next, they formulated a strategy. They did not have the luxury of simply waiting their turn in line to approach Jesus and receive his blessing. Scripture tells us there was no room left inside this home in Capernaum to get their friend to Jesus. Instead of giving up and becoming frustrated, they devised what must have been one of the most courageous strategies of their day to get their friend to the feet of Jesus. It was certainly an "outside the box" strategy. I can only imagine how far these four guys were stretched emotionally, physically, and spiritually to come up with such a plan.

When engaging in ministry partnerships, everyone involved must realize that newfound strategies will stretch you and take you beyond your comfort zone. That's why it's critical that we remember why we're doing it. If we can maintain the urgency of the need for young people to be reached for Jesus Christ, it keeps us from fighting as much about strategies.

Factor in Risk

The paralytic's friends displayed a high level of risky behavior. These guys defied the odds. "Since they could not get him to Jesus because of the crowd, they made an opening in the roof above Jesus and, after digging through it, lowered the mat the paralyzed man was lying on" (Mark 2:4). It doesn't seem that there was a whole lot of knee knocking going on. My guess is the knee knocking probably happened after they had lowered their friend in front of Jesus!

Ministering to young people is high-risk territory in and of itself. Add to that partnering with other youth ministries and Christian organizations from different cultures and socioeconomic backgrounds, and the risk factor quadruples. Youth ministers' behavior patterns must adjust to make room for the "high-tolerance leadership" that is needed.

The paralytic's four friends modeled how high-tolerance leadership works in high-pressure situations. Imagine the stares they received from the crowd, let alone the owner of the house! Well, you will need that same bold leadership if you are serious about youth ministry partnerships, because all eyes will be upon you, including those of the parents of the young people representing your prospective youth ministry areas.

Focus on the Ultimate Goal

While serving as the Young Life regional director in Chicago, God gave me a vision for creating a long-term, sustainable urban ministry model through involving various churches within my region. Local churches were excited about the possibilities of growing their youth ministry outreach into the community through a proven organization, and I began spending a large percentage of my time training and equipping youth pastors in local churches. In time we were able to locate and hire a full-time person to facilitate and oversee all that God was doing in this urban area.

Unfortunately, less than a year after the person was hired, and following countless hours of training and financial investment into this leader, he decided to leave. The news was shocking to everyone involved in the hiring process, and it took us a long time to regroup.

Yet in spite of the setback, several good things emerged from this unfortunate experience. For example, at the time of his resignation, several dozen kids were signed up to attend summer camp. Volunteer leaders provided ways for them to earn money through washing cars and other ventures, and the trip became a reality, with more than thirty of those campers committing their lives to Christ. That's the result youth ministry partnerships can bring, even when the human side of leadership gets in the way.

Those four unknown compassionate servants in Mark 2:1-12 had a clear goal in mind—to see their friend walk and run again. As a result, a new paradigm was introduced to the community that day; and no doubt the bystanders were in awe of these four friends' foresight, abilities, and teamwork tactics. There probably were several who said to themselves, "Why didn't we think of that?" It's this same attitude and focus that must be present in any youth minister today who is praying about partnering with other youth ministry organizations. Once such a spirit is present, the following partnership lessons are key to ministry success.

Key Principles for Effective Youth Ministry Partnerships

Surround Yourself With the Right People

One of my greatest joys during my years with Young Life was working in the Cabrini-Green housing project of Chicago alongside gifted, intelligent, and talented leaders who were committed to community transformation, such as Rev. Bill Leslie, senior pastor for more than twenty-five years at LaSalle Street Church. Bill, often referred to as "chaplain to the Windy City," had an appreciation and love for people that enabled him to create partnerships with other churches and parachurch organizations long before it was in vogue.

I observed firsthand as Bill's leadership and influence birthed six different partnering Christian organizations under the umbrella of LaSalle Street Church. Each of them was financially self-sustaining. It was, and remains, an incredible partnering ministry model for establishing effective collaborative efforts. Bill introduced me to many credible leaders who modeled for me how to conduct ministry under pressure without comprising one's calling, beliefs, or values. These mentoring relationships and many others guided my leadership for many years, and ultimately led me to my current position at Willow Creek Community Church.

Seek Leadership Support

As an urban youth minister, you have a front-row seat to just about everything that goes on within your community. You are constantly rubbing shoulders with pastors, high school principals, teachers, parents, organized criminals, local politicians, and others as you lead and serve young people. Youth ministers are uniquely poised to be some of the most strategic community organizers in any city!

In addition, many youth ministers in the "hood" are indigenous leaders who grew up on the very streets they now serve, so they are accustomed to the "survival of the fittest" lifestyle that's necessary for making things happen there. Network this sharp, aggressive, streetwise leader with a youth ministry organization that has resources and administrative structure but no affinity with life on the streets, and you have the potential for a powerful alliance. These intuitive leaders need senior leadership support, but not controlling dictators. They need to be empowered and trusted to get the job done in an efficient and effective manner, as they know better than anyone which youth ministries and organizations are the right fit for pursuing a potential partnering relationship with.

Create an Organizational Strategy

A long-term organizational strategy is essential for any organization or partnership to achieve success. Many urban youth ministers resist long-term planning, but without it long-term success just won't happen. The key is for those who are gifted managers to come alongside the more grass-roots urban youth workers and help them think through long-term strategies that are both doable and sustainable.

Incorporate Transferable Partnership Values

Within any culture, agreed-upon values play an important role in shaping behavior patterns. The same is true in the formation of youth ministry partnerships. It's critical that *kingdom organizations* live and minister by *kingdom values*. There are five transferable partnership values that I believe to be absolutely critical for the formation of successful youth ministry partnerships. They are community, evangelism, leadership, passion, and respect.

Community

When local leaders, residents, business people, and churches come together to focus on bettering their community, powerful things happen. Gathering together in focused smaller groups is the best way to make a larger impact. The same is true as we attempt to impact our communities through reaching young people with the gospel. Don't overlook this critical first step.

Evangelism

The Great Commission calls us to go and make disciples of all nations, baptizing them in the name of the Father, the Son, and the Holy Spirit. If your partnering pursuits neglect the element of evangelism, throw in the towel right now! This value must be number one in the minds of any Christian partnership desiring to impact urban teenagers.

Leadership

Any organization thriving in the twenty-first century must be diligent about the value of leadership. Here at Willow Creek Community Church we commonly hear, "Everything rises and falls on solid leadership."

Today's leaders are required to be multitask leaders, capable of juggling many balls in the air at the same time. Not only must we be able to lead in such a way, we must also pursue partnerships with other leaders who are capable of the same thing. We often paint unrealistic, rosy pictures for each other and then later discover we are not compatible to make the partnership work, which causes more harm than good in the end. Be sure you have gifted and complementary leadership in both parties.

Passion

One cannot overemphasize the value and need of passion. It is a contagious energy that calls others to sacrificially join the cause and helps to still the negative vibes that can quickly halt any movement. Partnerships are hard enough to accomplish in themselves, but a draining relationship between leaders and organizations can stop it in its tracks.

Respect

One of the biggest mistakes I have observed in the formation of partnerships is overlooking the value of respect. Effective coordination, collaboration, and community building take time, energy, and lots of human resources. If we don't take the time to build genuine, authentic relationships with one another, we will never develop the necessary respect that will be required when the attacks begin and the enthusiasm wanes. Do the necessary work on the front end to avoid disaster on the back end!

A Worthy Cause

There is nothing more exciting than seeing young people respond to the gospel, and nothing more effective than seeing diverse organizations bringing together their best and allowing God to meld them in a synergistic manner that produces something far more powerful than the sum of their parts. Don't give up on the sometimes difficult process of partnering with other youth ministries of different cultures. More than just reaching kids is at stake. Through a respectful blending, we also see a fuller realization of Jesus' prayer fulfilled: "May they be brought to complete unity to let the world know that you sent me and have loved them even as you have loved me" (John 17:23b).

Chapter 18
Nurturing Your Staff and Volunteers

Harvey F. Carey

O ne of the definitions the dictionary gives for *ministry* is "the filling of needs." This certainly fits the biblical example defined by Christ as he ministered to people—meeting their physical, social, and spiritual needs.

The needs are enormous among the children and youth who reside in our inner cities. No one youth worker can possibly begin to touch all of them alone. So let's settle this upfront. There is no place for lone rangers in the city. There is only one Messiah, and even he saw the need for developing and working through a team of people.

Even for those youth ministries large enough to employ multiple ministry staff, ministry volunteers are the strands that tie effective urban youth ministry together. No matter what the creative gifts of the leader, he or she will be able to reach only as far as the arms of the volunteer staff.

This chapter focuses on some proven methods for developing staff and volunteer youth workers in an urban setting. I don't claim to be an expert. However, after eleven years of full-time urban youth ministry, I have seen our youth grow both spiritually and numerically. We began with twelve teenagers in an urban community in the heart of Chicago and have grown to over twelve hundred. By God's Spirit, I credit the holistic caring for our youth, and especially our youth workers, as the primary reason for this growth.

But even as we develop volunteers and associate staff, they can easily burn out amidst the incredible demands and needs of the city. And how can we expect quality ministry from a team that is spiritually, emotionally, physically, and financially bankrupt? We can't! Retaining vibrant and effective youth workers requires instilling into them a sense of worth, value, and vision.

I define the soul as our will, intellect, and emotions. Caring for the soul of staff and volunteers, therefore, requires that we nurture not only their spirits, but also their thinking processes, their emotions, and their ability to make wise decisions. I have witnessed the fact that as a youth ministry intentionally cares for the souls of its leaders, it soon experiences prosperity in every other area as well.

Today's Urban Youth Ministry

Urban youth ministry faces many challenges from the impact of gangs, drug abuse, poverty, and dysfunctional families. However, not every urban young person comes from a background of unhealthy living. Many are in school and have families who are concerned and active in helping shape their futures for the better. As a result, we must recruit a variety of volunteers who can relate to and connect with many different kinds of urban kids if we're going to care for every young person who frequents our youth ministry programs.

While every teenager is different, all urban youth share a common need for love, concern, and commitment. Since many urban teenagers have been lied to often, it's vital that they find truth in Christian youth leaders who genuinely care for and about them. Thus, effective urban youth ministry begins at the point of recruitment. Such a task demands much wisdom and prayer. There must be a genuine calling to youth ministry on behalf of those we recruit. Urban youth ministry is not simply a committee they sign up for—our teenagers need committed, dedicated, and faithful workers.

Recruiting

Effective care for urban youth workers begins with how they are recruited. Rather than relying upon pulpit announcements and church bulletin advertising, I've found the most effective way to recruit is literally to recruit. This means personally approaching people and outlining your vision for them as youth leaders.

Parents, teachers, and other church members who are already actively involved in the lives of youth make great candidates for youth workers because their hearts are already in the ministry. It's important to give job descriptions, times of commitment, and any other requirements upfront so you will not have them feel as though you are "pulling any surprises" on them later. This is also a good way of caring for those who are called to youth ministry, because you are letting them know your expectations and limitations upfront, pre-venting burnout later.

Retaining

Retaining youth workers has a lot to do with their feelings of worth, value, and vision. When there is no direction or focus in youth ministry, youth work-ers ultimately perish. To safeguard against this, work hard to place your adult leaders in ministry opportunities that match their gifts and passions. This will give them opportunities to succeed, which is the greatest motivator of all.

In addition, find ways to celebrate them. Start by celebrating their call to the ministry. From the outset, have a ceremony to acknowledge the important ministerial role these people have, and have committed to. This shows them how significant their role is to the rest of the church body. Once they're on board, plan for regular times of celebration together. I'm not suggesting weekly feasts, but I am stressing the value of fellowship and food! Bring all your staff and volunteers together for a meal and a time of celebration through a slide show or silly games. This kind of celebration goes a long way.

Set up a system to regularly communicate with each of them. This can be done through e-mail, letters, phone calls, or leaders' meetings. Where there is little or no communication, staff and volunteers quickly feel out of the loop, become discouraged, and feel undervalued. And notice when they are miss-ing. Let them know that when they're absent your team isn't complete.

Lastly, just as cars, crops, and bodies need to rest, so do youth workers. Be careful that your workers are not feeling overextended or exhausted in ministry. It takes lots of effort to recruit and train them, so it's best to not risk losing them when all they may need is a little time off or a rotation of their responsibilities.

Recharging

Because youth workers are always serving, they rarely feel ministered to. A few years ago, we asked each of our youth to write letters to their youth workers, citing things the youth leaders did that impacted them in a power-ful way. We planned a getaway weekend for our leaders at a retreat facility a good distance from where our church is located. The church underwrote most of the expenses. We asked parents and others in the church to handle all the preparations for the weekend so our youth leaders could just enjoy one another and be celebrated. In that context we presented them with the letters as a climax to the retreat. Planning such times of refreshment lets our leaders know just how much we value their souls.

Another way of recharging youth workers is by providing them with good books, videos, and tapes that focus on developing their own spiritual depth as well as practical tools for effective youth ministry. Set up a resource library with such materials and encourage your leaders to make good use of it, for their sake as well as the health of your students.

Following Jesus' Example

While most of us derive great satisfaction from ministering directly with youth, the long-term fruit of our ministry is more closely tied to adequately caring for our adult leaders. It's why Jesus spent so much energy pouring his love and encouragement into his twelve disciples. And the impact continues today.

BV 4447 .C49 2002

City lights

Fax: (970) 679-4570

Evaluation for
City Lights

Please help Group Publishing, Inc., continue to provide innovative and useful resources for ministry. Please take a moment to fill out this evaluation and mail or fax it to us. Thanks!

● ● ●

1. As a whole, this book has been (circle one)

not very helpful   very helpful

1   2   9   10

2. The best

3. Ways this book could be improved:

4. Things I will change because of this book:

5. Other books I'd like to see Group publish in the future:

6. Would you be interested in field-testing future Group products and giving us your feedback? If so, please fill in the information below:

Name_____

Church Name _____

Denomination _____ Church Size_____

Church Address _____

City _____ State_____ ZIP _____

Church Phone _____

E-mail _____

Permission to photocopy this page granted for local church use.
Copyright © Group Publishing, Inc., P.O. Box 481, Loveland, CO 80539. www.grouppublishing.com